JESUS IN HIS TIME

JESUS IN HIS TIME

JOSEPH VOGT · ALBRECHT DIHLE
CARSTEN COLPE · BO REICKE
ABRAHAM SCHALIT · PAUL WINTER
KLAUS KOCH · HERBERT BRAUN
EDUARD LOHSE · JOSEF BLINZLER
ANTON VÖGTLE · WILLI MARXSEN
DIETER NÖRR · DIETER GEORGI
RUDOLF SCHNACKENBURG
HANS CONZELMANN

EDITED BY
Hans Jürgen Schultz

TRANSLATED BY
BRIAN WATCHORN

FOREWORD BY
William Neil

PHILADELPHIA **FORTRESS PRESS**

First English edition published in 1971 by S.P.C.K.

First American edition published in 1971 by Fortress Press

Second Printing 1972

Third Printing 1974

Translated by Brian Watchorn from *Die Zeit Jesu*, first published 1966 by Kreuz-Verlag GMBH, Stuttgart.

Quotations from the *Revised Standard Version* of the Bible, copyrighted 1946 and 1952 by the Division of Christian Education of the National Council of the Churches of Christ in the United States of America, are used by permission.

Library of Congress Catalog Card Number 70-99613
ISBN 0-8006-0163-7

4283A74 *Printed in the United States of America* 1-163

CONTENTS

NOTES ON CONTRIBUTORS

Joseph Vogt is Professor of Ancient History in the University of Tübingen.

Albrecht Dihle is Professor of Classics in the University of Cologne.

Carsten Colpe is Professor of the History of Religions, University of Göttingen.

Bo Reicke is Professor of New Testament in the University of Basel.

Abraham Schalit is Professor of Jewish History in the Hebrew University, Jerusalem.

Paul Winter is a Jewish writer on the New Testament and a contributor to the *Interpreter's Dictionary of the Bible*.

Klaus Koch is Professor of Old Testament in the University of Hamburg.

Herbert Braun is Professor of New Testament in the University of Mainz.

Eduard Lohse, formerly of the University of Göttingen, is Bishop of Hannover.

Josef Blinzler is Rector of the Roman Catholic Theologische Hochschule in Passau and Professor of New Testament.

Anton Vögtle is Professor of New Testament Literature and Exegesis and Roman Catholic Director of the Faculty of Theology Trier/Freiburg.

Willi Marxsen is Professor of New Testament in the University of Münster.

Dieter Nörr is Professor of Roman Law in the University of Münster.

Dieter Georgi is Professor of New Testament at the Divinity School of Harvard University.

Rudolf Schnackenburg is Professor of New Testament in the University of Wurzburg.

Hans Conzelmann is Professor of New Testament in the University of Göttingen.

Hans Jürgen Schultz is Chief Editor, Cultural Programmes, of the Süddeutscher Rundfunk, Stuttgart.

The Reverend Brian Watchorn is chaplain of Gonville and Caius College, Cambridge.

The Reverend Dr William Neil is Reader in Biblical Studies in the University of Nottingham.

FOREWORD

The ordinary reader picking up a book with an interesting title such as this might well be put off by the formidable list of contributors, most of whose names are unfamiliar—and German at that. He may be slightly reassured to learn that the contents of the book consist of talks originally given on German radio by a team of distinguished scholars, but designed for the general public and not for the theological specialist. Nevertheless, despite the widespread impact of the former Bishop of Woolwich's best-seller *Honest to God*, through which the names of Bonhoeffer, Bultmann, and Tillich became known to a greatly enlarged circle of readers as having something pertinent to say to our times, the old suspicion remains that German theologians are usually obscure and often incomprehensible.

We cannot forget W. S. Gilbert's humane Mikado's apt punishment for "all prosy dull society sinners, who chatter and bleat and bore" that they should be "sent to hear sermons from mystical Germans, who preach from ten to four". Nor, from another angle, have we had much encouragement from C. H. Spurgeon's memorable dismissal of the adventurous Higher Criticism which came from across the Channel at the end of the last century as "the German poison".

If it is a true description of some German theologians that they propagate extremist views couched in abstruse jargon, it would be an equally true description of some theologians who write in English. And in fairness to the Germans it must be said that they have too often been ill served by their translators. Let it therefore be clear from the outset that as far as this book is concerned the hesitant reader need have no fear. The translator has done a superb job and it is well-nigh impossible to detect that this is a translation at all.

But of course the chief credit for making this a stimulating, helpful, and eminently readable book must go to the sixteen contributors themselves. They have discarded the style which would be expected of them in articles in learned journals or in the lecture-rooms of their various Universities, and have successfully adjusted themselves to the simpler and more direct approach of broadcast talks which must hold the interest of the listener and make all the relevant points within the space of half an hour.

The authors, as can be seen from the Notes on Contributors on p. vii, are mainly University teachers in Germany. They comprise Protestants, Roman Catholics, and Jews with a preponderance of New Testament scholars, as befits the subject. There are, however, valuable contributions also from experts in Roman law and history, and in the civilization of the ancient world. Whether they exchanged notes on their contributions in advance or not, there is a remarkable unity of presentation, a natural sequence of subject matter, and hardly any overlapping.

The purpose of this series of talks was to illuminate the Gospel records by showing the background against which Jesus conducted his mission, and the Palestinian setting of his ministry amid all the social, political, and religious movements which affected his times. It is becoming more and more clear that Jesus, far from preaching an other-worldly message to simple peasants in an idyllic corner of the Levant, was himself inescapably involved in the harsh realities and tensions of a highly complex society, and that those among whom he worked, and to whose lives he sought to bring new depth and meaning, were as much involved in the pressures and crosscurrents of the times they lived in as we are ourselves today.

If we are to understand the gospel aright and its relevance for our day it is essential that we should see Jesus as he was in history: born in a small country which was terrorized by a mad tyrant, growing up under the repressive rule of a hostile occupying power, proclaiming the truth about God and man in a land which was rent with religious disputes and political turmoil, and which was subject to winds of change of extraordinary intensity. St Luke in his Gospel leaves us in no doubt that it was in such a setting—the world of Tiberius Caesar, Pontius Pilate, and the Herods—that Jesus had to take his stand and plead his cause.

There is much in this book that sheds new light upon all this, and much too that illuminates the references in the Gospels to the Jewish religious background—the dominating power of the Sadducees and the spiritual strength of the Pharisees, both employed in defence of orthodoxy, and side by side with them such sectarian movements as the recent discovery of the Dead Sea Scrolls has included in our knowledge of the true picture. We are told of the almost mystical significance of the Jerusalem Temple for Jews everywhere and of the role of the synagogue not only in the gospel story but as a channel of Christian missionary enterprise.

Were the disciples of Jesus in any way different from the disciples of other Jewish rabbis? Were the miracles of Jesus paralleled in other contemporary religions? What was the real point of the Last Supper and how was it related to eucharistic celebrations in the early Church? How was Christian missionary propaganda affected by the ideas and practices of the Gentile world? How were the death and resurrection of Jesus interpreted by his first followers and how can we interpret them today? These and other such questions are asked and all are competently dealt with.

Let it be emphasized again that this is not a book for the theological specialist but for all who wish to deepen their understanding of the New Testament and especially of the life and times of Jesus. It will prove to be of great assistance to all who are concerned with religious education—teachers, students, and clergy. The writers belong to no particular theological school of thought, left-wing or right-wing, radical or conservative. They write as objective scholars who have the gift of presenting their specialized knowledge in a way that not only illuminates the scriptures but also strengthens our faith.

University of Nottingham WILLIAM NEIL

1 Augustus and Tiberius

JOSEPH VOGT

It may seem surprising that a series about Jesus and his time should begin with two Roman emperors, Augustus and Tiberius. But both these names occur in the Gospel—Augustus for the dating of the birth of Jesus, Tiberius in connection with the appearance of John the Baptist and hence with the beginning of the public ministry of Jesus. Luke, who gives these details in his Gospel, uses the methods of a classical historian in other ways too; but here his concern is to place the life of Jesus within the framework of universal history. From the very first chapters of Luke's account the reader can see that in Jesus, whose genealogy is traced right back to Adam, God himself has entered the history of all mankind. The early Church, for which Luke writes, comprehends within its faith a universal drama of world events which runs from the Creation of the World through the Redemption of this time to the Judgement on the Last Day. In the middle of this span occurs the earthly existence of Jesus which impinges on Roman history and this gives a fixed chronological point which is confirmed by sources outside the Bible.

Augustus was the first Roman emperor and his achievement was that he brought to completion the worldwide rule of Rome. The great generals of the last years of the republic had carried the Roman eagle into vast new territories. Pompey had brought order to Asia Minor and Syria, Caesar had conquered Gaul as far as the Rhine. Augustus now completed the circle of Mediterranean countries by annexing Egypt in 30 B.C. Then he turned to the north and took the central Alps and the territory immediately to the north. His attempt to subjugate the Germans from east of the Rhine up to the Elbe ended in disaster in the Teutoburg Forest in A.D. 9. But the Rhine and Danube were secured as frontiers and afforded natural defences, as did the desert belt in Africa and Arabia to the south and the Euphrates in the east. It is true that the Romans had to come to terms with the existence of the Parthian empire in the east, and they also had some knowledge of India and China, but the countries and peoples which were now embraced by Roman rule were in effect regarded as the entire world. Rome ruled the world (*patrocinium orbis terrae*).

Augustus' contemporaries hailed him for bringing the empire to completion. But they were even more grateful to him for creating peace at home than for success in war. For a hundred years Rome and Italy had been rent by civil wars. The organs of the republic— the assembly of the people, the senate, the annually elected magistrates—had become dependent on generals who were all powerful. Now the last of them had brought off the remarkable feat of combining the institutions of the republic with personal leadership of the state. After the turbulent years of his youth, he had in his maturity found a way of reconciling all the political groups and on the basis of his undisputed authority had established an autocracy. He then took the title of honour by which we know him: Augustus, the illustrious, and was accorded that godlike veneration which the ancient world believed was due to a man of creative talent, to a man endowed with charisma.

There was indeed some opposition to the first "princeps", and it was bound to appear doubtful to those who looked further ahead whether this personal achievement could outlive the man who created it. But in his long reign Augustus did an enormous amount to secure peace both at home and throughout the empire. He consolidated the social orders of the Roman people and led the citizenry back to the old religion and the ways of their forefathers. "Because you show due reverence to the gods, you rule on earth", says the poet Horace of the Roman who has recovered his old identity. The subjects in the provinces were also to share in the blessings of the imperial peace, the *Pax Augusta*. The administration of the provinces by governors appointed by the emperor and the senate was brought under strict regulation, and the indigenous upper class was encouraged to participate in local government in the newly won northern territories as much as in the old cities of the Greek east. This desire for order on the part of the imperial government had its effect even outside the empire. Numerous princes beyond the frontiers, Arabians as well as Germans, were brought under Roman suzerainty. They ruled as representatives under the protection of the emperor, as clients of Rome. So the principle was now accepted in the Roman world of establishing law and order, encouraging travel and trade, and of securing peace.

Not surprisingly, this beneficent policy of Augustus was welcomed by both citizens and provincial subjects. Roman poets and artists hailed the reign of the first emperor as a golden age. The whole history of Rome was thought of as an arduous rise to power under the fate of Jupiter, now completed by the achievement of Augustus. As the poet Vergil declares:

> This is the man, this is the one whom you have long been promised,
> Augustus Caesar, offspring of a god, founder of the golden age.[1]

They went still further in the Greek cities of Asia. There the emperor's birthday was elevated to the beginning of the calendar year, for, as we are told in the decree of a provincial assembly: "Providence has graciously sent him to us and to the generations after us to be our saviour ... the birthday of the god was the beginning for the world of the glad tidings brought by him." Even the Jews, who abhorred the cult of a ruler, reverenced this emperor. Philo of Alexandria writes in a long string of praises of Augustus: "This is he, the princeps Augustus, who saved the whole human race, whom men fitly call the averter of evil."

It is true that Philo writes from within the context of the Jewish *diaspora*. But Palestine too, the holy land of the Jews, had become part of the Roman empire after a long period of unsettlement. Pompey had intervened with armed force in the struggle between the last members of the dynasty which had emerged from the Maccabean revolt. Caesar had been concerned for the welfare of the Jews and had granted them many privileges. And in the end Palestine had become a protectorate of the Roman empire. Herod, who later—and misleadingly—was given the name "The Great", had been appointed king and, confirmed by Augustus, ruled the country with violence and terror from 37 to 4 B.C. He was a friend of the Romans, founded the city of Caesarea on the Palestinian coast in Hellenistic fashion in honour of the emperor, and, despite all his atrocities, put the Jews in his debt by building a magnificent new Temple in Jerusalem. After his death there were violent

[1] *Aeneid* vi. *791-2*

disturbances which were put down by the governor of the neighbouring province of Syria, and Augustus divided the various districts of
Palestine among the sons of Herod. Archelaus, the eldest, was given
the central area, Judea, but he ruled so brutally that after ten years
Augustus had to send him into exile. So in A.D. 6 Judea was put
under the direct administration of the Romans, and the small
province was given a governor who bore the title of *praefectus* or
procurator and was subordinate to the imperial legate in Syria.
Caesarea became the governor's residence and the garrison for
Roman troops, with only one of the five cohorts stationed in Jerusalem. This ancient holy city was the seat of the Sanhedrin, the
supreme council, which was the highest spiritual authority for all
Jews throughout the world, and for Israelites in Judea exercised
jurisdiction over religious matters. Relations between the Jews with
their strict beliefs and the Gentile occupation force were always
tense, though the Romans abided by the privileges granted the
Jews, did not insist on their participation in the ruler cult, and were
at pains to remain at a distance from their utterly strange, monotheistic religion. Augustus expressly commended his grandson Gaius
for not offering sacrifice in Jerusalem when on his way through
Judea to the east.

This, then, is the historical framework which it is Luke's intention
to give to the birth of Jesus:

> In those days a decree went out from Caesar Augustus that all the
> world should be enrolled. This was the first enrolment, when Quiri-
> nius was governor of Syria. And all went to be enrolled, each to his
> own city. And Joseph also went up from Galilee, from the city of
> Nazareth, to Judea, to the city of David, which is called Bethlehem,
> because he was of the house and lineage of David . . ." (2.1–4).

For over a century this birth narrative of Luke's has been the
subject of intense historical and theological investigation. We shall
confine ourselves to the historical problem, and in particular to the
question of which year it is to which these verses refer. It certainly
cannot be the first year of our era, as was thought by Dionysius
Exiguus, a monk of the sixth century, whose calculation was later
used to fix the Christian era. For this much is generally agreed,
that Jesus was born in the last years of king Herod and so, at the
latest, in 4 B.C. But could Augustus have ordered a census in Herod's

territory while the king was still on the throne? Does not the name of Quirinius, the governor of Syria, point to a completely different year? We have information about this able commander and governor, Publius Sulpicius Quirinius, from sources outside the Bible; and we know that he became governor of Syria in A.D. 6 and that in this capacity he had an enrolment or census taken in Judea at the time when the country became a province. It is clear that an enumeration of this sort was made with every new province in order to provide information for taxation. As we learn from the better-known case of Egypt, the people were required to register for this purpose at the place to which they belonged. Many scholars have therefore concluded that Luke made a mistake in connecting the date of Jesus' birth with the census taken when the province was created. This sounds plausible, but it is not at all certain. An inscription from Tivoli and the short biographical sketch which the historian Tacitus gives of Quirinius suggest that he had already been imperial legate in Syria a good ten years earlier, and in this position had conducted a war against a tribe in the Taurus Mountains. It is not impossible that it was then that he was ordered to take a census in the territory belonging to the vassal-king Herod. There is no doubt that occasionally the Romans did take such measures outside their frontiers, and the idea of annexing this territory may have already been under consideration in the last years of Herod, when he became more and more dependent on the Romans. Perhaps one day a new inscription, papyrus, or coin will throw more light on this first tenure of office of Quirinius. Meanwhile, we can give only a probable date for Jesus' birth, and it seems that the best case can be made out for 6 B.C.

Roman presence as a world power is an important theme in Luke's narrative: for instance, he fixes the appearance of John the Baptist to the fifteenth year of the emperor Tiberius, and merely by this dating gives a hint of the light and shade of the *imperium Romanum* as it was experienced in the small province of Judea. Those who have not entirely forgotten the sharply defined characters of the first emperors will carry a mental picture of Tiberius, who succeeded Augustus in A.D. 14. Tacitus characterized him as the archetypal despot, but recent research has given us an insight into the tragic story of a remarkable person. There is no doubt that he was a great general and a prudent statesman, but a harsh personal fate prevented him from fulfilling the same messianic hopes that

Rome had held of his predecessor. Tiberius was in fact the first victim of the principate—that marvellous but extremely dangerous form of personal government. Augustus began early to train a successor, but in the delicate play of family politics his stepson Tiberius was always only a minor character, and only after the others had died was he chosen for the lead. He began to reign at the age of fifty-six, a greatly disappointed and disillusioned man. With the seriousness of the Claudii from whom he was descended, he saw the position of emperor as service of the state and took pains to uphold the constitution as he understood it. He became the ascetic of the principate, strict to other members of the imperial family, inaccessible to the people of Rome, distrustful of the senate, and, above all, dissatisfied with himself. He created ill will for himself by his lack of assurance, which amounted in effect to a sense of his own worthlessness, and generated that mixture of opposition and servility in the Roman upper class which led to a long series of treason trials. He was so sickened by the servility which he saw around him that he withdrew from public affairs and allowed, and even encouraged, the prefect of the guard, Sejanus, to seize power and forge his way by craft and violence to complete control. From A.D. 27 Tiberius, the ruler of the world, lived in his refuge on the Isle of Capri and left Sejanus in control to become all powerful. In the end he succeeded in getting rid of this dangerous evil genius but, now deprived of his last confidence in others, Tiberius became a morose tyrant. Murders and informing are characteristics of the final struggle between the princeps and the aristocracy of Rome.

A Roman general once remonstrated with the refractory subjects of a province on how well off they were to be so far from harm's reach with a tyrant as emperor. Under Tiberius too the provinces were well off. This was not just because the affairs of the city of Rome did not affect them, but also because the positive character-istics of the emperor came to the fore in provincial government. Tiberius was credited even by Tacitus with thrifty financial man-agement and conscientious administration of justice in his early years; in the provinces this opinion of him never changed. The emperor sent out able governors and kept them in office for long periods in the conviction that it was better for the people if they were not exposed every year to new bouts of exploitation. Once, when the prefect of Egypt remitted a larger sum in taxes than was required, the emperor reprimanded him with the words: "a good shepherd must shear his sheep but not fleece them".

Even Judea had years of comparative peace in this period: *sub Tiberio quies*, says Tacitus in his survey of the conflicts between the Jews and the Romans. Perhaps Sejanus was hostile to the Jews. We have some evidence to suggest that in his last years he wanted to compel the emperor to take action against them. Certainly the governor sent to Palestine in A.D. 26 was no friend of the Jews. This was Pontius Pilate whom we know not only from the Gospels but also from Jewish and Gentile sources. A few years ago a dedicatory inscription of his was found during excavations at Caesarea, in which he styles himself *praefectus Iudaeae*. The Jewish writers, Philo and Flavius Josephus, picture him as an arrogant, unjust, cruel master. They tell us how, contrary to all custom, he was determined to have the standards, decorated with their pictures of the emperor, and the shields of honour, inscribed with the emperor's name, carried into the holy city, and how he requisitioned the temple treasure for the construction of an aqueduct. In this way the hostile feeling between the Jews and the Roman administration was kept very much alive.

These then are the circumstances relating to the emperor, the empire, and the province to which the factual statement of Luke introduces us when he dates the appearance of John the Baptist:

> In the fifteenth year of the reign of Tiberius Caesar, Pontius Pilate being governor of Judea, and Herod being tetrarch of Galilee, and his brother Philip being tetrarch of the region of Ituraea and Trachonitis, and Lysanias tetrarch of Abilene, in the high-priesthood of Annas and Caiaphas . . . (3.1–2).

We have a whole set of synchronisms here, and yet only the fifteenth year of Tiberius can be at all precisely dated and that not with entire certainty. On one reckoning this fifteenth year runs from August A.D. 28 to August A.D. 29, on another from October 1 A.D. 27 to September 30 A.D. 28. If we are content to take the year 28 as the date of the Baptist's first appearance, we also have a date for the beginning of the public ministry of Jesus. The detail given later in Luke (3.23) that Jesus was at that time "about thirty years old" fits in well with the date we assumed for his birth. But it is a contested question how long this public ministry lasted. At least

two years are probably required by the Gospel accounts. So we arrive
at A.D. 30 as the year of his death.

Later chapters will deal with Jesus' message, his disciples, and his
opponents. Let me just sketch in here how Roman might impinged
on the last days of Jesus' ministry as this appears to the historian
in the light of current scholarship. In his book *The Life and Death
of Jesus of Nazareth*, the American writer Joel Carmichael interprets
Jesus as a rebel against Rome, and his band of disciples as a group
of resistance fighters. This is a profound misunderstanding even
though the author does refer to the methods of modern scholarship.
It is quite clear that questions of the power of the state are given
only incidental attention in Jesus' preaching. Even the saying about
taxes paid to Caesar and about the tribute money subordinates the
political question to the expectation of the kingdom of God. But the
entry into Jerusalem and the cleansing of the Temple do represent
an open attack on the spiritual leaders of the Jewish people. It is
the Jewish authorities who are responsible for Jesus' arrest, and their
supreme council which interrogates the accused and sentences him
to death on the charge of blasphemy. Jesus has to be handed over to
the governor for the sentence to be ratified and executed. At the
proceedings before Pontius Pilate the charge is one of political sedition; the Jews put pressure on Pilate who is undecided: "If you
release this man, you are not Caesar's friend." So Pilate pronounces
the death sentence from the judgement-seat and has it carried out
by Roman soldiers. The political basis of the sentence is indicated
by the inscription fixed to the cross: Jesus of Nazareth, king of the
Jews. Only a charge of rebellion had any chance of succeeding before the governor, and in those years of treason trials, of informing
and of murder, he was certain to be convicted. Pilate was afraid
that information would be laid before the emperor against himself,
alleging that he had released a man guilty of treason. His hand was
forced, and then he got his own back with the inscription: this is
the sort of king you deserve.

Presumably Pilate made a report on the trial to the emperor
Tiberius. There is a story in later Christian writing that, when
Tiberius received this report, he submitted a motion to the senate,
but without success, that they allow the worship of Christ. This is
a piece of pious fabrication which probably originated in the second
century and was meant to show the emperors of that period how
good had been the relations under their predecessors between the

Roman state and the new religion. In the Julio-Claudian period, when the emperor and his officials had to deal with Christians, they must have regarded them in much the same way as did Tacitus when he endorsed the action taken under Nero against the Christians in Rome.

These people who are hated for their abominations are commonly called Christians. Christus, from whom the name is derived, was executed in the reign of Tiberius by a procurator, Pontius Pilate. But this plague was checked only for a moment, for it broke out again in Judea and spread as far as Rome—a pernicious superstition.[1]

[1] *Annals xv. 44*

2 The Graeco-Roman Background

ALBRECHT DIHLE

The places which feature in Jesus' ministry were part of that great land-mass around the eastern Mediterranean which was opened up to Greek civilization by the conquests of Alexander the Great in the fourth century B.C. and which remained open to that influence for many centuries afterwards by becoming part of the Roman empire in the first century B.C. In Syria and Palestine, as elsewhere, Alexander and his successors founded numerous cities where the way of life was Greek. In comparison with them, only a few urban centres managed to retain their native language and culture, such as Jerusalem or Edessa in northern Syria, while the Aramaic-speaking population in the countryside was scarcely involved in what went on in the world at large.

In the Hellenistic period, that is, in the centuries after Alexander, and within the Roman empire, Greek culture in the eastern Mediterranean was quite literally a civilization, for it was created by the citizens of these Hellenistic cities. Although the cities were almost always part of a territorial state ruled over by a monarch, they still had their own laws, religion, and calendar, conducted their own affairs through elected civil servants, and depended on taxes raised from their own citizens. This autonomy of the community preserved the political independence of the classical Greek city-state, as well as encouraging a civic sense which found expression in numerous public institutions, in the founding of schools, theatres, and sports arenas, and also in a rich community life. All this had a strong attraction for the surrounding indigenous people for whom the Greek language and way of life was for centuries the prescribed route to social advance. The fact that later on it was primarily in the cities that Christianity spread is in keeping with the urban character of Graeco-Roman culture; and so is the way the early Church was organized on the basis of city bishoprics. Up until a late date the rural population continued to be culturally under-privileged.

The Greek city was a centre of considerable independence which allowed its citizens to feel very much at home. At the same time the world in which they lived was not at all parochial. In earlier days the individual had been tied for better or worse to the family or community of his forebears. But now, after Alexander's conquests, there were wider possibilities. A craftsman from Ephesus could try to make a new life for himself at Alexandria in Egypt or at Antioch in Syria. The governments of the great empires recruited their experts from throughout the world, as did their armies and seats of education and learning. Trading was also highly organized, reaching as far as India and Britain, and was facilitated by an equally developed monetary and credit system. Thus many people were well aware of the existence of an extensive world outside, which, in actual fact, was within their reach.

The Greeks were skilful at opening up territories which had become theirs by means of techniques of progressive rationalization. Then the political stability brought by the Romans for a long time protected the feats of engineering and organization which have such a modern ring about them, although there were hardly any new developments after the second century B.C. The same is true of science where the position reached in the third century B.C.—in mathematics and medicine for instance—was generally maintained until the great crisis of the third century A.D. Much of it was not then improved on until the nineteenth century. This extensive world with its mobile society and highly developed technical equipment continually demonstrated to people that they could make better and more successful lives for themselves by disregarding the old conventions and by using their own intelligence, although this might mean taking risks which were hard to calculate. These circumstances were related to certain distinctive religious and moral attitudes which were to be important for nascent Christianity.

The Greeks in earlier times sacrificed to gods who rewarded this service by taking the family or community under their protection, dispensing fertility and good fortune, and guaranteeing the continued existence of the community. So no social unit was possible without a centralized cult. These gods, however, were not responsible for people outside the community which sacrificed to them; neither did they give ear to the private concerns of the individual. It is true that there was scarcely any need for such individual piety as long as the individual was a member of a familiar community governed by the settled ways of their forebears. But all this changed after the time of Alexander. A man from Corinth who wanted to move to Syria the next day and whose brother lived in Egypt could hardly pray to the god of just one city. And the more his life moved outside the sphere to which his forebears had adhered, the more he had to meet situations in his life without the help of well-tried conventions. If he was not to feel that he was the mere pawn of fate or *Tyche*, he needed a divine helper who was concerned for him personally.

The result was that the old religions of city and state continued to have some meaning as the expressions of community feeling, but the hearts of the people turned to gods to whom they could pray in the community of like-minded believers anywhere. Participation in this sort of cult, not bound up with the community, was not part and parcel of the old conventions of social and political life, and so these cultic groups which were scattered among the cities stood in need of some order and organization and no doubt of a developed pattern of belief too, in order to give a clearer interpretation of the cult's activity than that afforded by a local saga or a half-remembered tradition. In fact this gave reason for recruiting new members to particular cults—reason, that is, for practising mission.

The gods who were worshipped by these congregations originated partly in Greece. This, for instance, is the case with Aesculapius, who had already become a god to whom the individual turned outside city cults for help in time of sickness. Characteristically, his great rise to popularity begins within the scope of the Hellenistic world. The mystery cults, esoteric cults which had existed in Greece for generations and promised a limited number of initiates blessedness in this life or immortality in the next, were particularly suited for the new form of community.

And finally, a group of cults whose expansion in the Greek world is a particular feature of the period, namely the worship of oriental gods, such as Isis from Egypt, Cybele from Anatolia, Tammuz from Syria, or Mithras from Persia, also shared the character of mystery religions. Presumably these cults usually spread first through merchants, mercenaries, or slaves who had come from the east and had settled in Greek cities. There they continued to practise the cult of their homeland and in this way came to the notice of their neighbours. As these religions attracted adherents of widely different origins and outgrew their native environments, there grew up religious congregations which were not confined to any particular region. They had developed rituals, explanatory mythologies which were often well-thought-out theologically, and an established hierarchical ordering of the group. All of them afforded direct communion with the god, the lord of the cult, usually in crude ceremonies which brought joyous release from the limitations and cares of everyday life as well as the assurance that the individual would be preserved after death. The ancient and often strange-sounding myths, which gave an explanation of the sacred meals, washings, mortifications, processions, or dances, were expounded as descriptions of the fate of the world and of the soul of man, both of which found salvation in the acts and sufferings of the god, for salvation could be regularly re-enacted in the cult and mediated to believers. These cultic congregations with their fixed form of organization offered their believers a place where they could feel at home in a world which had become too big for them. In fact, by going through more and more steps of initiation they could also satisfy their desire for social advancement.

It is clear that many of the features I have mentioned found their way into Christianity: direct communion with the deity in the cult, the social significance of congregational life, the theological interpretation of cult and myth. Even so, none of the mystery cults in the Hellenistic and Roman worlds ever made any claim to be exclusive, and none of them developed a code of ethics for daily living in addition to regulations for cultic purity. The omission in this respect in Hellenistic religious life calls for an explanation, particularly if the social significance of these new religions is taken seriously. It goes without saying that other forms of irrational aspiration after salvation and security—such as astrology among the upper classes and magic among the lower classes—also had no ethical norms for daily living.

It is necessary for our answer to look to philosophy, which had a greater influence on the general moral ideas of the time than we can appreciate from the position in our own society. In the fourth century B.C., the age of Plato and Aristotle, philosophy had taken on a new surge of life. The foundations laid at this time were built on in the Hellenistic period to produce the intellectual framework of several rival schools of thought. The result was that philosophy came to be regarded not so much as an unceasing investigation but as the systematic ordering of empirical knowledge about the world and mankind from which one went on to derive moral principles by strict logic. The purpose of this philosophy was to acquire ethical standards rationally. So it more or less exactly matched the rational and technical conquest of the material world which we mentioned previously, though it seems to be at variance with the popularity of the extremely irrational piety of the cults.

This rational ethic had far-reaching influence for several reasons. For one thing, it became the practice for centuries to devote a part of all higher education to philosophy, often in fact by going to study in Athens, which was the acknowledged centre of philosophical learning. In addition, many educated people made a habit of seeking advice from a counsellor or confessor trained in philosophy before making grave and difficult decisions. And now that the whole of public life was in the hands of prosperous, educated citizens, it was inevitable that principles of philosophic ethics should permeate the legal and administrative systems.

But the influence of philosophy went even further, for there were professional philosophers who attached no importance to the scholarly basis of philosophy. They concentrated entirely on giving practical guidance for living and addressed themselves in edifying lectures and personal conversations directly to the man in the street. Philosophers were highly regarded by both rich and poor and the considerable differences between their schools naturally became blurred as their tenets were popularized. We can, then, talk of a homogeneous ethic of popular philosophy which was widely adopted in the Hellenistic and Roman period and was characterized by the following principles.

The end of all human effort is the moral perfection of the individual, not the welfare of society. True, man is a member of society, but that conformity to society's ethical requirements, which is the basis of community, has meaning only because in this way the individual develops the talents which nature has given him. This emphasis on the moral autonomy of the individual—for whom only nature, and no social group, sets moral standards, and whom no one, as a result, can relieve of moral responsibility—possibly produced the best fruits of classical culture. The moral autonomy of the individual is complemented by the idea of the equality of all men as brothers. The differences between Greek and non-Greek, slave and free, rich and poor, may be important socially, but morally they are irrelevant. It is clear what an important corrective this doctrine brought into a culture which exhibited extreme differences of class. Lastly, this code of ethics did not rely on divine wisdom which was revealed to elect persons only. It was understood as the logical consequence of rational insight into the nature of man and could therefore be discussed. Since it was in no way tied up with any particular religion, it could be linked with all kinds of piety without losing its rational and humanitarian character.

This ethic was able to hold its own for something like two hundred years in the settled conditions of the Roman empire where an educated, well-to-do bourgeoisie set the tone, and this despite the fact that, although the ethic was handed down as something taken for granted, it received no further development because speculative interest turned to other subjects. For this reason it showed little capacity for assimilation when the great crisis of the third century A.D. put power into the hands of the new, less educated strata of the populace and led to that barbarization of moral ideas which goes to make up the more repulsive side of the culture of the Middle Ages. Elements of the old humanitarian ethic survived only where they were interpreted as the content of religious teaching, as happened in Christianity.

At the time of Jesus, this ethic of popular philosophy was still a dominating factor in Graeco-Roman civilization. Love for all mankind had, of course, its limits. Marked differences in status and education saw to that, as well as the predominantly commercial attitude of the urban bourgeoisie. But there is scarcely any other period in the history of the world when public and private life for so long exhibited such tolerance, moderation, and enlightenment. This was really the most valuable contribution made by philosophy to Graeco-Roman civilization.

As for the influence of philosophy on religious ideas, it consistently led the educated to a monotheism which conceived of the guiding force of the universe as an impersonal god. The thinking of the later Hellenistic period, which was more interested in speculation than empiricism, developed further the idea that all cults and myths contained a partial knowledge of the true nature of God, if only it were interpreted correctly, that is, allegorically. So the stories of classical literature, the legends of local cults, and even the strange practices of oriental religions were interpreted throughout to give symbolic statements about the cosmos and the fate of the soul; for Greek influence still predominated in that there was a continual attempt to view man in relation to the totality of nature. This flexibility in manipulating theological concepts, which seems strange to us but which was taken over only too readily by Christianity as well as by the traditional forms of cult, was able in the end to justify every religion and combine it with the basic moral principles of the civilized world. In these circumstances Christianity had great difficulty in maintaining its claim to be exclusive, which it had inherited from the Old Testament tradition. Only by defining more and more sharply the idea of orthodoxy and, on top of this, naively equating right belief with right morality was it able to make headway in a world which was as accustomed to a variety of religions as to the uniformity of moral thinking independent of religion.

In the world of Greek civilization a considerable part of the population was made up of Jews scattered widely among the cities. They had begun to spread around the Mediterranean much earlier, favoured by many circumstances in the Hellenistic and Roman period. The Greek intelligentsia at first felt sympathy and interest in Judaism. They thought that the strong monotheism of the Old Testament corresponded to the philosophical concept of God, and that the law of the Jewish community realized the ideal of rule by philosophers. For their part, the Jews became remarkably quickly assimilated to the Greeks in language and culture, but without giving up their religion. By the third century B.C., the Old Testament was being translated into Greek and at the same time the Jews began to develop a rich literature in which they interpreted their own traditions in terms of Greek philosophy and history. This attests the incorporation of a conscious Jewishness into Hellenistic culture. We know of Jews who played a notable role in the literary life of the first century B.C., and we also hear of conversions to Judaism. It was also inevitable that the teaching of the synagogue should in more than one respect become assimilated to popular philosophy, for the law was read in Greek and interpreted in the light of concepts taken from Greek philosophy.

For a time it seemed as though even Palestine, which, because of Jerusalem, was the religious centre of Judaism, would be opened up to Greek culture and language. But the Maccabean revolt in the second century B.C., sparked off by encroachments from the Seleucids who were then the supreme power, hardened the anti-Hellenist position. Nor did the Romans manage to incorporate this country into their culture beyond annexing it into their empire. The active, intellectual life of Palestine, unlike that of the *diaspora*, continued to centre on the Jewish tradition, and the Hebrew text of the Old Testament was expounded in the Aramaic vernacular, not in Greek. Any confrontation with Greek thought was avoided, though in everyday life use was made of Greek, even when dealing with their co-religionists from all parts of the world. The basic cause of the ferocity with which the two Jewish wars of the first and second centuries A.D. were fought was that the traditions of the two parties were thus so very alien to one another.

But the Bar-Kochba revolt, which was the final catastrophe for Palestinian Judaism, also dealt a mortal blow to the Greek-speaking *diaspora*, for their flourishing existence was founded on the assumption that the Jewish religion and way of life could be contained within Graeco-Roman culture. The ban on missionary activity in the Roman state and the drying-up of Jewish Greek literature in the second century A.D. mark the end of a long and promising development of which Christianity was the heir. Christianity had at first spread through the Roman empire chiefly as a teaching in the Greek synagogue-communities. But by the second century it was sufficiently independent not to be hit by the catastrophe in Judaism. But the infiltration of Greek philosophical concepts into the new religion, which helped Christianity make its impact on history, followed the lines laid down by Hellenistic Judaism.

The impact of Jesus can be understood historically only against the background of his country's Judaism, which on the surface had become part of the Graeco-Roman world but at bottom was completely estranged from it. We know, however, of this impact only from sources written in Greek which at every turn betray Hellenistic concepts, though in varying degrees. So it is surely no accident that it is those sayings of Jesus in particular which take issue with the Jews' sense of election and replace pious self-concern with unconditional love of one's neighbour that come to the fore in the tradition handed down to us. True, the service of one's neighbour in Jesus' teaching has a different basis from that of the humanitarianism of Greek philosophy. But both concepts led to similar results in practice. And if anything in later antiquity gave Christianity the edge

over other religions which promised salvation for the soul, it was
the entirely new fusion of religion and morality effected in Jesus'
teaching. Unlike other forms of cultic piety in the ancient world,
early Christianity gave a religious justification to the moral requirements of everyday life. These requirements in themselves were not
unknown to Graeco-Roman civilization, but, because of this new
religious justification, they had an effect in the life of the Christian
congregations which made a deep impression on the surrounding
world.

3 East and West

CARSTEN COLPE

In the first chapter the historical setting was deliberately confined to the reigns of Augustus and Tiberius, and then in the second was widened to take in the Hellenistic and Roman world surrounding Palestine. We are now going to expand the historical setting to the dimensions of world history, as they were then thought to be. From the historical and political angle this larger setting can be characterized by the conflict between the Romans and the Parthians, and from the religious angle by the conflict and fusion in the Hellenistic world between so-called Graeco-Roman traditions and those called oriental.

What was this power which in the first century B.C. appeared on the borders of a Roman empire which had already conquered the Near East and was shortly to be consolidated by Augustus? The rise of this power can be seen as part of the same process which led to the inevitable collapse of the Seleucid empire and to the emergence of the Greek kingdom of Bactria in the east, the kingdom of Pergamon in Asia Minor, and the Hasmonean kingdom in Palestine. Though the Achaemenid empire had been destroyed by Alexander the Great, the Seleucids had retained in their territory its system of satraps in all its essentials. Already under the Achaemenids the post of satrap and that of the hyparch under him had become hereditary. This development continued under the Seleucids, so that eventually the whole of their empire was made up of principalities which were more or less independent. The satraps or hyparchs had power over internal, military, and economic affairs, while the cities which, like military colonies, were supposed to be directly dependent on the king, were in practice very largely autonomous. In general these local dynasties, which often had a pronounced feudal character, were left to their own devices by the Seleucid rulers as long as taxes and other levies came in regularly and the great trade routes between the Mediterranean and central Asia, which were so important for both the prosperity and the cohesion of their empire, were protected and kept open. One of the territories which eventually became independent and shook off even the nominal supremacy of the Seleucids was the province of Parthava to the south-east of the Caspian Sea. About the middle of the third century B.C. this area had been infiltrated by a branch of the great Scythian tribe of the Dahae—the Parni as they were called, who previously had wandered as nomads between the Caspian Sea and the Aral Sea. The name of the province was then taken over by the tribe which had moved into it.

These events are closely connected in time and substance with the revolt of Bactria. The first Parthian ruler Arsaces (Arshak) is said to have been governor of the Bactrian Greeks. He is supposed to have risen in rebellion and to have fled to the west to set up his own kingdom. The historical facts behind this tradition are probably that the satrap of Parthia, apparently a man called Andragoras who is depicted on various coins, rose in revolt at about the same time as the Bactrian Greeks but was in turn overthrown by the Parni under the leadership of Arsaces. At any rate, it is this Arsaces (whose name has now been authenticated from outside Greek tradition by a potsherd from Nisa in what is now Turkmenistan) who has given his name to the Parthian dynasty, the Arsacids. In addition a host of legends has collected around him, like those we know of other founders of Persian dynasties. They need not concern us here. The Arsacids began their expansion with the conquest of the neighbouring country to the north-west, Hyrcania. This was not something which the Seleucids could idly let happen. And so the way was paved for a long succession of military reprisals and Parthian revolts in the course of which the sphere of Arsacid rule was slowly extended.

The power destined to play a significant role in history and merit the name of the Parthian empire was not established until the reign of Arsaces VI (also called Mithradates I). His reign began between 170 and 160 B.C., which is more or less the same time as the Maccabees in the west rose against the Seleucids. He compelled some other feudal lords in the Persian highlands to recognize his sovereignty or replaced them with men from his own following. In this way he became ruler over what was once Media, whose traditions were later to have a lasting influence on the Parthians, and also over the principality of Elymais with its old capital of Susa, which had been formed on the territory of the old Elamite kingdom. The rich city of Seleucia on the Tigris, the former capital of the Seleucids, apparently considered it politic to make a settlement with the Parthians. Opposite the city, on the left bank of the Tigris, the Parthians built a large military camp where Mithradates set up court. Out of it later grew Ctesiphon, the capital of the Parthian empire. Mithradates considerably extended the civil service, brought in improved legislation and introduced the Attic currency. On his coins he called himself "Philhellen", not least because he remained dependent on the support of the Greek cities; for the feudal lords of Media and South Persia, particularly in Persis, the ancient country where the Achaemenids originated, on the one hand considered themselves to be rivals of the Arsacids and on the other took every opportunity to show that they preferred the rule of the Seleucids to theirs. And when the Greek kingdom of Bactria began to decline, the north-east Persian tribe of the Sacas came to be a serious threat to their borders.

Not until Mithradates II (123–88/87 B.C.) could the empire be kept secure. He settled the Sacas and was probably recognized by them as their king. Thus the Parthian empire stretched in the east as far as the borders of India, including what is now Kandahar. In the west he reconquered Mesopotamia where during the reign of his predecessor the new state of Characene had been founded by Hyspaosines in opposition to the Parthian governors. Within this enormous area the caravan trade went on undisturbed and prospered. The most important route was part of the famous silk-route. The trading-post with the Chinese merchants was at a place which is usually identified as Tash Kurghan on the upper Yarkand. From there the route ran through Bactria (where hostile Kushan tribes frequently made it unsafe), on to Raghae, the ancient Rai, and then through Ecbatana–Hamadan either to the oasis of Palmyra or to Dura–Europos on the upper Euphrates.

Mithradates was in a position to take the title "King of Kings" and to have a relief cut in the rock of Behistun, not far from the inscription of the great Achaemenid Darius, which shows him receiving homage from his commander-in-chief and from three other feudal lords. One of these figures perhaps symbolizes the subjugation of

3

Great Armenia where Mithradates had extended his influence towards the end of his reign and where he took as a hostage a young prince, who was ultimately to be made king by him and become Tigranes the Great of Armenia.

The remarkably widespread occurrence of the name Mithradates, "the one given by [the god] Mithras", presents a problem for the history of religion, about which we shall be talking later. His most outstanding namesake in his time was King Mithradates VI, Eupator of Pontus (120–63 B.C.). He was the last Hellenistic opponent to be a serious obstacle to the Romans in their march east. Mithradates of Parthia kept out of this struggle, but Tigranes of Armenia made a treaty with Mithradates of Pontus, and after the death of the Arsacid king, which as usual was followed by a struggle for the throne, he seized several Parthian provinces. The enforced neutrality of the Arsacids made it possible for the Romans under Lucullus to defeat Tigranes in 74 B.C. When Lucullus was forced to retreat by a mutiny among his troops, the Roman senate replaced him by Pompey, who went on to conquer the whole of Syria and Palestine including Jerusalem (63 B.C.). Mithradates of Pontus was pushed back into his territories in southern Russia. His son Pharnaces, who had attempted to stage a recovery by invading Bithynia, was defeated by Caesar at Zela in Pontus in 47 B.C. This was the event which Caesar reported in his famous words "veni, vidi, vici". Only then, when Caesar had recovered the provinces of Asia Minor, was the last resistance west of the Euphrates eliminated.

But the enemy east of the Euphrates, the Parthians, could not be eliminated. Crassus the proconsul, the man who in 56 B.C. had joined with Pompey and Caesar as the third member of the second Triumvirate, as it is called (or rather, acceded to Caesar's attempts to renew the Triumvirate from 60 B.C. by being reconciled with Pompey), marched east from Syria which had fallen to him in the allocation of the provinces, and crossed the Euphrates. But at Carrhae his legions were almost completely wiped out by the Parthian cavalry (this was in 53 B.C., ten years after Jerusalem had been taken by Pompey). This event marks a turning point in the history of relations between east and west in this period. Before Carrhae, the Romans had taken scarcely any notice of the Parthians. After Carrhae the Parthians featured so strongly in the Roman consciousness that Greek and Latin writers virtually divided the world into a Roman half and a Parthian half. This resulted in contemporary historians writing even about Parthian affairs which had no direct connection with Roman history. In this way, through the writings of Cassius Dio, Josephus, and Tacitus, we have a fairly comprehensive picture of Parthian history from 69 B.C. to A.D. 72, and so in the time of Jesus too. The earlier period is supplemented by the account of Pompeius Trogus, which goes down to 9 B.C., though the years 94–55 B.C. are missing owing to the carelessness of his epitomist Justinus. Plutarch's biography of Crassus is also an important historical source.

The native sources of Parthian history are more meagre. They are primarily inscriptions and coins. We have already mentioned one of the ostraca from Nisa, the ancient royal city of Parthia, which come from the period 100–29 B.C. At first the coins are in Greek style and do not begin to give the date until 37 B.C. Not until the reign of King Volagases I (A.D. 51–80) do the initials of the kings' names appear in a local script on Arsacid drachmas. Subsequently there are a number of longer inscriptions on coins, on walls, and on various objects. Finally, important information is furnished by archaeology. There is a distinctive Parthian style of building and sculpture, which is seen at its best in the Arab city-state of Hatra, which the Arsacids employed as a buffer state against the Romans. In particular the gods of this temple–city must be mentioned. In style as well as in iconography many of them still resemble their Greek precursors, but their inscriptions are all written in the Aramaic dialect of Hatra. The proper names these give are naturally the most interesting material of all. The mother-goddess occurs under the names of the Babylonian Nanaya and the Syrian Atargatis, and the ways in which she is depicted sometimes bear a likeness to representations of the old Arab goddess Allat, at others to Aphrodite or Venus, or again to Artemis. The weather god in the form of Jupiter or Zeus looks like the north-west Semitic Hadad, and a puzzling god called Simios, Simia, or Semaia, "the heavens", reminds us of Aesculapius or Hermes. Most interestingly, all three are also linked together in a triad as "Our Lord, our Lady, and the Son of our Lords". Moreover, we find the widespread Semitic sun-god Shamash in the form of Helios or Sol and a sinister chthonian deity with the stylistic traits of the Greek Hades, the axe of the Babylonian Nergal, and the robe and snake of the Iranian Ahriman.

These commingled deities reveal at their starkest both the conflict and the fusion between east and west. But a completely different picture of the many-sided relationship between the two spheres is given by the Judaism of this period.

The Arsacid administration had already come across Jewish communities in Hyrcania, and after 160 B.C. came up against the Jews in Babylonia who had lived there since the Exile and had not returned to Palestine under Zerubbabel, Nehemiah, and Ezra. This colony was so strong that it must be regarded as the centre of Jewish national history right until the tenth century A.D., particularly after the Roman conquest of Jerusalem had caused a further influx of Jews to this colony. While the Palestinian Jews eventually reacted against Seleucid rule by rising in revolt under the Maccabees, the Babylonian Jews at more or less the same time gladly accepted Parthian rule, and the Parthians for their part realized that by treating the Jews well they could win the good will of their fellow-Jews in Palestine who shared their wish to be rid of Seleucid domination. Thus it was that Alexander Jannaeus (104–78 B.C.) received a Parthian delegation which, significantly, is not mentioned by Josephus, who was sympathetic to Rome, but only by the first tractate of the Palestinian Talmud. Later the Jews and Parthians were bound together by common opposition to Rome. So there developed lively contacts between the Jews of Palestine with their centre at Jerusalem and the Jews of Babylonia with their large communities at Nehardea, Nisibis, Machosa, Pumbedith, and Sura. The Babylonian Jews went to the great pilgrim festivals at Jerusalem and were made welcome there; the Palestinian Jews lent support to their brethren in Parthian Babylonia, Media, and elsewhere, with delegations and letters about matters of faith, cult, and law, among them some by great teachers such as Gamaliel I, Jochanan ben Zakkai, and Simeon ben Gamaliel. Jewish influence became so great that between A.D. 35 and 40 Adiabene, a Parthian tributary state on the upper Tigris, was converted to Judaism through its queen, Helena, and her two sons, Izates and Monobazos. Thereafter this dynasty made rich offerings to the Temple in Jerusalem, and in the north of the city they had a magnificent burial-place built which still exists in a well-preserved condition. Princes from Adiabene later gave military support to the Jews in the war of A.D. 66–70 against the Romans.

The conflict between the Romans and Parthians marks a turning point in history, and for this reason other important details deserve mention. But the subsequent political history, the Parthian wars of

Mark Antony, Octavian, Tiberius, Nero, Trajan, and Septimius Severus, the emergence of collateral lines of the Arsacids, the Persian reaction against Hellenism in the Parthian empire, the gradual decline of Arsacid power and its overthrow by the Sassanids—all this cannot be pursued in a study of Jesus and his time. More important for our inquiry are the numerous small states between the Roman and Parthian empires where the conflict between the two took on definite shape in both culture and religion, and found expression in very varied forms of syncretism, cultural assimilation, or pluralism. After the fall of Tigranes the Great had given rise to bitter differences between the Parthians and Romans over Armenia, Arsacid princes occupied the throne of Armenia from the beginning of the Christian era well into the period of the Sassanids. Apart from the kingdom of Pontus, already mentioned, a whole host of problems for Graeco-Iranian history is posed in Asia Minor by Cappadocia and Commagene in particular. The same is true of the small kingdoms of Osrhoëne in north-west Mesopotamia with their capital at Edessa and also of the territories of Adiabene and Hatra, to which we have just referred. In the south of Mesopotamia we have already mentioned the principality of Characene (or Mesene) which extended around the mouth of the Tigris and Euphrates and also for a time quite a distance to the north. Finally, we must also include with certain qualifications, the oasis of Palmyra, which at times came under Parthian influence politically as well as culturally. Palestine, however, was not one of them, although Antigonus, the last of the Hasmonean kings, received help from the Parthians to recover the throne of his fathers (40–37 B.C.) after the Roman senate had already appointed Herod as king.

As far as Parthian or Graeco–Roman influence is concerned, the problem for the history of religion and culture in the first century A.D. and the last century B.C. is concentrated on these particular countries. But there is in addition a whole set of other influences making the problem really complex. The most important are the Iranian influence (Iranian, that is, in the wider sense which is not simply identical with the Parthian), the Babylonian influence, that of Asia Minor, the west Semitic, and the Egyptian. But none of these contributes to the syncretism of the late classical world by itself, that is, separate from the Greek factor, but every one of them is mediated through the Greek factor. For this reason it is useless to ask whether Hellenism, which we are dealing with as a phenomenon

of the history of religion and culture, should be defined as Greek
culture corrupted by the east or as oriental culture which has
become adapted to the Greek world. Neither the oriental nor the
Greek elements can be separated from the entity of Hellenism, which
is more than the sum of all its parts. This fact also unfortunately
puts in question the dominance of the Parthian element, which it
would be nice to see as a more precise phenomenon in the history
of religion than the frequently cited "Iranian influence" on Greek
and Hellenistic culture and on Judaism, which scholars at one time
found it necessary to talk about.

From some of the small states mentioned we have details of their
ideology of kingship. In Pontus it is tied up with the birth and
upbringing of Mithradates Eupator, in Armenian chronicles with
the burial ritual, in Commagene with the religious policy of king
Antiochus I, by Arab historians with the coronation of the Sassanid
ruler in which perhaps were preserved some Parthian customs.
Discoveries and excavations in Asia Minor, as well as in many
Persian areas, have brought to light fire-shrines, including, for
example, one at Nurabad which was built in Parthian times but
incorporated very many older ones. We know the temples of Kurkha
and Kangavar. The historian Appian describes a great sacrifice
offered by Mithradates Eupator in Zela and the geographer Strabo
describes a large number of sacrificial practices. We also learn from
him a great deal about the priesthood of the Magi, among whom
the Median influence mentioned above is most apparent (the Median
tribe of the Magu were the priestly caste of the ancient Median
empire). Apocalyptic writings have come down to us such as the
Oracle of Hystaspes and all sorts of apocalyptic material of the
Sassanids, which indicates that there was a Parthian apocalyptic.
We know, lastly, legends about a redeemer, which may have a
Parthian background, and we know the fully developed religion
of the mysteries of Mithras.

But how much of this is Parthian, and how much not, depends
on how we define Parthian, and while this is easily done with the
material of political history, it is difficult to do with the material
of the history of religion. There is no clear way of telling even
within the boundaries of the Parthian empire itself when and where
we are dealing chiefly with Greek or Iranian influence. So like the
minor states we have mentioned, as well as the sometimes older
Hellenistic kingdoms and even eventually the *imperium Romanum*

which was superimposed upon them in the west, the Parthian empire itself represents the immense historic dynamism caused by the conflict between east and west which even modern scholarship cannot neatly resolve.

Only pragmatic historical investigation will wish to draw from these facts anything which is of consequence for the time of Jesus in its narrower sense. The Parthian kings on the throne in this period —their names and dates are known but are not relevant here—did not make sufficiently great a mark on history, even when they were in direct conflict with the emperors Augustus and Tiberius, for some knowledge of them to be necessary for an understanding of details in the New Testament or its background. The description of the events surrounding the birth of Jesus with the visit of the magi to Bethlehem or the spiritual armour in the Epistle to the Ephesians may have been based on Parthian models, but this is of no consequence for their substance. Gnosticism, which was to interact mutually with early Christianity in such complicated ways, originated partly in the Parthian world, but it also had roots in so many other areas that it must be regarded as more than a Parthian phenomenon. Jewish apocalyptic shows many points of similarity with Iranian apocalyptic, but this can easily be explained from circumstances within Palestine, so that it can be argued conversely that the situation there influenced Iranian apocalyptic and so must have begun to have an effect in the Parthian period. Our conclusion is that we cannot derive from the conflict between east and west any precise conclusions or theories relevant to what happened in the time of Jesus. What we have here is in fact background material. But it is perhaps this which (as at any period) allows the true originality of the really new to stand out for what it is.

4 Galilee and Judea

BO REICKE

In biblical times the Holy Land was united politically only under David and Solomon and again under the Hasmoneans and Herod in the last two centuries B.C. Otherwise Palestine was divided into various territories. After the death of Herod the Jewish kingdom again split up and was divided among three of his sons. They were Herod Antipas, Philip, and Archelaus. Herod Antipas, who was Jesus' sovereign, acquired Galilee and Perea (south Trans-Jordan) and reigned over these territories until A.D. 39. Philip governed north Trans-Jordan with his capital at Caesarea until his death in A.D. 34. Archelaus was given the historically important parts of the country, Judea and Samaria, but in A.D. 6 was deposed by Augustus. Augustus then put Judea and Samaria under a Roman governor or procurator who had his residence at Caesarea on the coast.

Jesus was connected principally with Galilee and Judea. Galilee was his homeland. In Jesus' time it was largely Jewish in population and religion. But this was a recent development. After the Assyrians had conquered the Northern Kingdom of Israel in 722 B.C., Galilee had acquired a Gentile population. Arameans and other peoples had migrated there, which is why St Matthew speaks quite correctly of Galilee of the Gentiles (4.15). In 104 B.C., however, the Hasmonean king, Aristobulus I, made Galilee a dependency of Judea and the people in Galilee were judaized to a remarkable extent. In the first century B.C. many Jewish families emigrated to Galilee. Jesus himself provides an instance of how families from Judea settled in Galilee. For Jesus' family is traced back in Matthew and Luke to Judah and David; Joseph and Mary had certain connections with Bethlehem in Judah, and in the Gospels Jesus is always represented as a Jew, never as a foreigner. Another example of Jewish influence in Galilee is the reaction of the people against the Hellenistic buildings put up by Antipas for a new capital, Tiberias, which he decided to build on the western shore of the Sea of Galilee. The devout Jews reacted against the idea and refused to live in Tiberias, because it was the site of an old burial ground. Because of this Tiberias was regarded as unclean, and so it acquired a Hellenistic population or, at least, one which was not strict in observing Jewish law. Jesus and his disciples also appear not to have been to Tiberias; the Gospels mention the city only in passing. A third instance of how important the Jewish presence was in Galilee is the fact that the Zealot movement originated in Galilee. This was a fanatical group made up of men who were zealous for the Jewish law and opposed Hellenism and the Roman presence with violence. Galilee also had a large number of Jewish synagogues and in post-biblical times became the centre of rabbinic Judaism. It was in fact Tiberias where the Jewish legal experts worked who later produced the Masoretic text of the Bible and made the collection of laws which are in the Mishnah. Galilee at the time of Jesus and his apostles can therefore be regarded as a largely Jewish country and only to a certain extent as still Gentile.

Josephus, the Jewish historian, describes Galilee as an extremely fertile and intensively cultivated area which looked like a magnificent garden. The most fertile part is the plain of Gennesaret, where Jesus' public ministry began. Gennesaret is a coastal strip about three miles long and only a mile wide on the north-western shore of the Sea of Galilee. The climate is subtropical and the plain is protected from the wind by high hills. Trade was a large source of income, for the important caravan route which ran from Damascus through Naphtali to Caesarea on the coast passed through Gennesaret. Capernaum was a military station and customs post on this trade route. A little further to the south there was an important centre of industry, the city of Magdala or Tarichea. There the fishermen sold their catch made in the exceptionally well-stocked lake. It was then salted and exported abroad. The Galilean fishermen formed co-operatives, owned expensive equipment and must not be thought of as uncivilized or illiterate individuals but as suppliers for a food industry. Farming, trading, and fishing flourished therefore in Galilee, and the Hellenistic buildings of Antipas are evidence of a high level of material culture.

Religious life centred on the synagogues, over which Jewish scribes exercised a certain amount of supervision. Secular government was in the hands of Antipas, although he remained dependent on Augustus and Tiberius. In official matters he was at pains to show consideration to the Jewish scribes and Pharisees. For instance, he minted coins without images and put in an appearance at the great religious festivals in Jerusalem. But personally he was a Hellenist, and when he dissolved his marriage with a princess from the neighbouring country of the Nabateans and married his ambitious sister-in-law, Herodias, he came into conflict not only with the Nabatean king but also with the pious Jews. John the Baptist, who was an embarrassing critic and a champion of the godly, was beheaded, but the Nabatean king declared war against Antipas and a few years after the death of Jesus defeated him. Because of this and other irritations the emperor deposed Antipas and Herodias in A.D. 39 and banished them to Lyons.

The area which was once the principality of Antipas and Herodias looks fabulously beautiful to the modern traveller, especially in spring. Jesus preached in this delightful countryside and told men of a new earth. The earthly to him was a hint of the heavenly, and the flowers of the field, the farmers, and the fishermen were used by him in his parables of the kingdom.

Judea, in contrast to idyllic Galilee, is a dramatic, grey, and wild country. The landscape continually alternates between hill and valley. Heaven and hell seem to be about to join battle in nature. The places of significance in the history of religion—Bethel, Jerusalem, Bethlehem, and Hebron—lie on a precipitous ridge which runs from north to south and rises to 2500 feet at Jerusalem and 3000 feet at Hebron, while not far east the surface of the Dead Sea lies 1300 feet below sea-level.

The Roman province of Judea, where Jesus was active at the end of his life, was made up of ancient Judah, together with Idumea, formerly Edom in the south, and Samaria, the larger part of the former Northern Kingdom of Israel. Judea, being hill-country, was not naturally rich, and fertile areas really only existed around Jerusalem and Hebron, in the Jordan valley, and on the plain of Sharon. But Jerusalem, Joppa, Lydda, and Jericho were also important as trading cities. Unlike Galilee, Samaria had never been amenable to the great religious traditions of Judea. So Samaria formed a largely heathen enclave between Judea and Galilee, much to the Jews' annoyance. In the post-exilic period the Samaritans had built a syncretistic temple on Mount Gerizim, urban civilization in Samaria was largely Hellenistic, and economically the country was richer than Judea.

After Archelaus, at the request of the Jews, had been deposed in A.D. 6 and Judea placed under a procuratorship for the first time, Augustus made the procurator reside at Caesarea, the magnificent new port on the Mediterranean founded by Herod. It was built in Hellenistic style and steeped in Hellenistic culture. Augustus also had a Roman enumeration or registration for taxation taken in Judea and Samaria around A.D. 6. This was supervised, we are told, by the governor of the province of Syria, Quirinius. We hear of this registration, or one like it, in Luke's birth narrative. It meant that the people of Judea and Samaria had to declare their means to the Roman authorities. Since it principally involved land taxes, the Jews had to make their declaration in the place where they owned land. Perhaps Jesus' parents went to Bethlehem, the city of David, because they had land near there. Not everyone in the country showed such loyalty during Quirinius' enumeration. It provoked opposition which began in Galilee and led to the development of the Zealot party. But the Roman soldiers stationed in Judea were able to quell the disturbance and continue the enumeration.

The Roman governor or procurator in Caesarea on the coast was the financial agent of Augustus. This means that his particular duty was to exact taxes and channel them into the imperial treasury. He had in his service tax-collectors who must be seen either as independent operators or as agents of such operators. They paid in to the authorities a lump sum, but how they exacted the imposts was their own business. An instance of a Jewish tax-collector who was one of these operators is Zacchaeus in Jericho. In Luke he is called a chief tax-collector, which means that he in turn had agents in his employment. The Jewish tax-collectors were not therefore state officials but private operators and like their agents had every opportunity to feather their own nests at the expense of the people. But this was not the only reason why tax-collectors were regularly lumped together with sinners. Jewish tax-collectors were hated so intensely because they carried on their disagreeable employment on behalf of a Gentile regime. The procurator at Caesarea had military support to ensure that these taxes could be levied in peace. These were not Roman legions but auxiliaries from the east. In his military capacity the procurator can perhaps be compared to a regimental colonel. He had under his command five cohorts, each of them consisting of about 600 men. Jerusalem had a cohort permanently stationed in the fortress of Antonia which was in the north-western corner of the Temple area, and from there it was easy to control the crowds and the Temple activity. Apart from this the procurator's troops were stationed mainly in Caesarea on the coast. Whenever the procurator went up to Jerusalem for the pilgrimage festivals, which seemed important for him to do in case there were disturbances, he was escorted by a cohort from Caesarea and took up quarters in the Praetorium, that is, Herod's palace in the western part of Jerusalem. It was the soldiers of the procurator's escort who had to see to the crucifixion of Jesus.

The internal administration of the country, however, was largely in the hands of the Jews. It is true that the procurator was responsible to Augustus and represented a high court of appeal for the Jews. But in the legal system and in administration the Jewish local authorities had a responsibility of their own. Self-government of this sort was normal in the Roman empire. Following a Hellenistic pattern the Holy Land was treated like a *polis*, with Jerusalem at the centre as the capital. And the supreme council in Jerusalem was treated as a counterpart to Hellenistic assemblies of citizens or to the Roman senate. The official correspondence of the Romans with the Jews was addressed to "the government, senate, and people of Jerusalem". The supreme council in Jerusalem was originally made up, like the senate, of elders or patricians, which is why Josephus, writing of the period about 200 B.C., talks of a *gerousia* or "assembly of elders". After the death of Herod I this assembly of elders was reorganized with the permission of Quirinius. Its first new leader was the high priest Annas, also known to us from the Gospels. Annas became high priest in A.D. 6 and, even after he had been deposed in A.D. 15, continued to control Jewish politics until his death *c.* A.D. 35. Most of his successors were members of his own family, including Caiaphas, his son-in-law, and five of his sons too. At the time of Jesus the Roman procurator had the right of nominating the high priest, and this meant that there was a quite frequent change of holder of the office. But as regards internal politics, the high priest was still the most powerful man in the land, for he was chairman of the supreme council by virtue of his office.

According to the Mishnah tractate Sanhedrin, the supreme council consisted of seventy-one persons. Meetings were held in a hall west of the Temple area, the councillors wearing their robes and sitting in semi-circles as in a theatre. There were committee meetings as well as general meetings. The New Testament mentions three groups in connection with the supreme council: the high priests, the elders, and the scribes. This agrees with the composition of the supreme council as we know it from rabbinic sources. When high priests in the plural are mentioned, this does not mean all the former high priests still living but a consortium of eight to ten men, composed of the high priest in office at the time, the priest in charge of the Temple as his deputy, a few priests from the nobility, and some financial experts. This was the executive committee of the supreme council which, as the government of the Jews, was responsible for daily business. Not the least important in this committee was the last group mentioned, the treasurers, for they were experts in financial matters, and the Temple finances had become very complicated owing to the great turnover in goods and in cash. So the consortium of high priests constituted a Jewish supreme authority whose members had to be available in the Temple almost every day. The second grouping in the supreme council, the elders, was unable to be present to the same extent. These were patricians who as land-owners had much else to do apart from politics in Jerusalem. In earlier days the supreme council was perhaps akin to a House of Lords, but by the time of Jesus this was no longer the case. In New Testament times the members of the third group, the scribes, played a role which was sometimes of decisive importance alongside the high priests, for the matters that had to be dealt with became ever more difficult. As the word "scribe" indicates, they were men of academic training. Their studies covered theology and law, for the sacred law was fundamental to the administration of justice. Ezra was the great exemplar for the scribes, and in the post-exilic period they had increasingly acquired greater importance. Their duties included the administration of justice, teaching, and instruction in wisdom. The leading scribes, whether they were followers of the Sadducean or Pharisaic school, taught students who either intended to become scribes themselves or wanted the religious education of a citizen. Paul had been one of these students; we are told that he sat at the feet of the famous Pharisaic jurist, Gamaliel. The phrase refers to the fact that the students squatted on the floor while the teacher sat on a stool. The scribes were held in great admiration by the people and carried the title of rabbi. This Aramaic word is derived, like the Latin *magister*, from the adjective meaning "great".

Of all these functions of the supreme council, its fundamental responsibility was the supervision of the Temple and sacrifices. The high priest was supposed to see to the conduct of worship, but mostly this was done by the chief priest of the Temple, assisted by a group of priests who were on Temple duty for a week at a time. The great expense of maintaining the Temple buildings, sacrifices, and priesthood was met by taxes and gifts. Most important of all was the annual Temple tax sent to Jerusalem from all over the ancient world. This was levied on all Jewish men over twenty, with the exception of the priests, and amounted to half a shekel or a stater per annum. In New Testament times this was the equivalent of a double drachma and today would be about a dollar. Temple monies had to be paid in the old Tyrian currency, which is why those money-changers were needed whom we hear of in the Cleansing of the Temple.

The supreme authority of the Jews as well as that of the Romans was involved in the arrest and trial of Jesus. The chief priest of the Temple and the Temple police under him made the arrest. After the trial before the high priests, Jesus was handed over to the Roman procurator with a petition for his execution. The name of this official was Pontius Pilate, a name which has been immortalized by the Apostles' Creed. He was the fifth in the succession of seven procurators in the first procuratorship. Pilate was not a member of the higher nobility, but like the other Roman procurators belonged to the equestrian order, the second social group of the Roman empire. The members of this class were mainly business people but, if they wanted to make a political career, posts like that of procurator of Judea were open to them from the time of Augustus. The highest positions to which the knights could climb were the prefectship of Egypt and the supreme command of the Imperial Guard in Rome. Pontius Pilate was appointed procurator of Judea in A.D. 26 by Sejanus, the commander of the Praetorian Guard. Under Tiberius this notorious tyrant was allowed to conduct political affairs almost independently. His political conceptions were based on an ideal of Roman sovereignty. Pilate enthusiastically pursued the same ideal in Judea. Soon after his appointment he ordered the cohort which was due to take up duty in the citadel at Jerusalem to march into the city with their Roman standards, although images were forbidden there. The Jews were incensed and flocked in crowds to Caesarea where they managed to persuade the procurator to rescind the order. One of Pilate's creditable acts was the construction of an aqueduct from the region of Bethlehem to Jerusalem. The Jews demonstrated against this too, but Pilate succeeded in getting the work finished with the help of soldiers dressed as civilians, and remains of the aqueduct can still be seen. The fact that c. A.D. 33 Pilate was persuaded to execute Jesus may also be connected with his idea of sovereignty. But by that time he no longer had the backing of Sejanus, and during his last years Jewish opposition to him grew stronger. A few years after the crucifixion of Jesus, when Stephen was martyred in A.D. 36, Pilate was no longer procurator. The governor of Syria had dismissed him because the Jewish upper class was too strongly opposed to him. But Pilate had successors, and the Jews were ruled by the governors of the first procuratorship until A.D. 41.

The administration of Judea was a particularly difficult problem for the Romans. It is true that Augustus had created the first procuratorship, lasting from A.D. 6 to 41, at the request of the Jewish nobility, for they preferred to be ruled by the emperor than by the Herodians. But Roman taxation and the policies of the procurators continually created tension. The old days of freedom under the Hasmoneans and Herod looked more and more rosy, and messianic or Zealot movements among the people created all sorts of disturbances. The Acts of the Apostles and Josephus show us that in the time of Jesus and his apostles there sprang up a score of messianic claimants and Zealot agitators. The proclamation from Galilee of the kingdom of God was easily mistaken by outsiders for a political movement. Jesus was crucified instead of an agitator called Barabbas, and Paul was later taken for a notorious assassin, nicknamed the Egyptian. It is evident that at the time of Jesus Judea was rife with political tension. It came as a surprise to the authorities to hear Jesus say to Pilate, "My kingdom is not of this world."

5 Herod and his Successors

ABRAHAM SCHALIT

If we were to assess the historical significance of king Herod entirely from the view of him given by the accounts in Talmudic tradition, we could not help regarding his reign as an insignificant interlude of no consequence whatever in the chequered history of the second Jewish state. The information we have of this great Idumean occupant of the Jewish throne from the entire voluminous literature of the Talmud is both meagre and distorted by legend. We hear of a Hasmonean princess, the only member of her family not to have been murdered by the "Hasmonean slave", Herod, who escaped from being murdered too by throwing herself from the roof. Herod then placed her corpse in honey and assaulted her (compare the same theme in the story of Melissa, the wife of Periander of Corinth: Herodotus v. 92). Following this odd story, we read a bizarre conversation between Herod and Rabbi ben Buta, who had been blinded by him; finally, Herod's Temple building is fleetingly mentioned in legendary terms. And that is all the Talmud has to say about Herod. Talmudic tradition obviously tries to make out that Herod was an ephemeral phenomenon in the history of the second Temple, who disappeared from the scene of his activity leaving no traces behind him. But appearances are deceptive. The truth is that the rabbis were well aware of the real significance of the sinister figure of the Idumean, but they concealed what they knew for reasons of their own just as, for similar motives, they chose to forget the historical facts which led to the great war against Rome and the destruction of Jerusalem and, sixty-two years later, to the war of Bar-Kochba which, if anything, was more terrible still.

In the eyes of the modern historian the reign of Herod is a momentous stage in the disastrous administration of Judea by Rome and clearly forms an historic watershed. On the one side, the rise of Herod finally brings to an end the national independence of the Jewish people which had been won by the Hasmoneans and maintained for more than a century. On the other side, the reign of Herod marks the beginning of severe internal disaffection in Judea, the cause of which is not difficult to find. This usurper, appointed and protected by Rome, opened the eyes of the people of Judea to the fact that the rule of their own prince high priests, which had gone on for centuries and had become sacred to the people, was now definitely over and that its place had been taken by the "impious regime" of the Gentile world power embodied in the hated figure of the "Hasmonean slave" and "half-Jew", Herod. The fact that Herod's reign was also the beginning of Gentile rule over Israel made him appear like an Egyptian plague in the eyes of the people, if not indeed like some kind of apocalyptic event, for his reign was interpreted as the beginning of the messianic woes. The reign of Herod thus provides the historian with a means to understanding the religious and social unrest in Judea during the last seventy years of the second Temple, inasmuch as it was the breeding ground for all sorts of messianic and apocalyptic currents. These were suppressed with an iron fist during the king's lifetime, but immediately after his death they burst all the more forcefully through the constraints which had been set on them, carrying away the poor and the oppressed who were longing for social justice and the political liberation of the nation. It is the whole of this development which I intend to sketch in broad outline in this short survey of the reign of Herod and his successors.

The young Herod's début in public, shortly after he had been appointed governor of Galilee by his father Antipater, gave the people some idea of what kind of man he was. He captured a band of Galilean terrorists who had been harassing the Syrians with their raids (Josephus quite wrongly calls them "robbers", as the Romans would) and had them put to death on the spot without trial. Arbitrary action like this carried the death penalty in Jewish law, so he was called to defend himself before the highest Jewish authority in Jerusalem, the Great Sanhedrin, the head of which was the high priest. Confident of the friendship of Sextus Caesar, the governor of Syria at that time, and escorted by an armed guard which he took for protection on the advice of his father, he went to Jerusalem to present himself before the court. This brazen action of his so

4

intimidated the judges that they did not dare to examine him, let alone pass sentence against him. But one member of the court, the famous scribe Sameas, resolutely persisted and, when it seemed that the law was after all going to take its course, Herod fled from the city, helped by the president of the Sanhedrin, the high priest Hyrcanus, who dreaded Herod's being convicted because he had been warned by Sextus Caesar not to pass a death sentence against his protégé. But Herod was not content with this outcome to the trial and soon afterwards appeared before Jerusalem at the head of a band of troops, fully determined to force his way into the city and punish his enemies. It was only with the greatest difficulty that his father and his elder brother Phasael, who held the office of governor of the city, were able to persuade him to withdraw.

Right from the start, then, Herod openly appeared as a partisan of the Romans, basing his political future exclusively on Rome and treating the Jewish authorities with contempt, the high priest not excepted. He kept in mind the political principle of his father, which was to serve whichever Romans were in power, no matter what political ends they wished to pursue, and to stick at nothing in holding his ground once it had been won. So Herod was quite un-scrupulous in cultivating friendships with anyone of importance in Rome whom he happened to meet and in dropping them as soon as their power was at an end in order to ingratiate himself with who-ever had replaced them. Thus he faithfully supported Cassius, the Republican, one of the murderers of Caesar, when he came to the east to raise money and troops for the fight against the dictator's heirs. Then after the battle of Philippi we see him smartly going over to the victor, Mark Antony, with whom power now lay, and adjusting to the new political star. He succeeded not only in driving from the field his Jewish accusers who hoped to set the triumvir against Herod, but also in increasing his power quite considerably, for along with his brother Phasael he was raised to the rank of tetrarch. Despite the hatred which surrounded him, his prestige rapidly increased, especially after he had averted the attempt of Antigonus, a Hasmonean and the younger son of Aristobulus II, to invade Galilee. A further apparent achievement, which was, how-ever, to prove later to be a disastrous mistake, was his engagement to the Hasmonean Mariamne, the granddaughter of the high priest, Hyrcanus.

The fateful year in Herod's life was without doubt 40 B.C., when the Parthians invaded Syria. The Hasmonean pretender to the throne, Antigonus, threw in his lot with them and succeeded in getting his claim to the throne of Judea recognized by the commander-in-chief of the Parthian invasion army, occupied Jerusalem, and shut up Herod and his brother Phasael as well as the high priest Hyrcanus in the citadel of the Hasmoneans. Phasael and Hyrcanus were lured into a trap. The former, it appears, was killed in fight, while the latter had his ears cut off and was taken into captivity by the Parthians. But Herod managed to escape with his family, among them his fiancée and his mother. He fled first to Egypt and from there to Rome to his protector Antony. At Antony's suggestion, and with the agreement of Octavian, the senate appointed Herod king of Judea by the grace of Rome. But that was all the help Rome would give Herod for the time being. The new client-king would himself have to resolve the problem of how to deal with his opponent, the protégé of the Parthians. Herod's task was not easy in view of the hostile attitude of the people of Judea, and the likelihood of his succeeding was for a long time very dubious. How unpropitious Herod's task was is apparent from the fact that in the third year of the struggle he had to call in the help of Antony whose legions finally produced a decision in favour of Herod. In the late summer of 37 B.C. Jerusalem was taken, after a courageous defence, by the Roman general Sosius and was handed over to Herod as the capital of his kingdom. The defeated Hasmonean, Antigonus, was beheaded at Antioch on the order of Mark Antony.

Even so, fighting against Herod was far from ended. The people of Judea entered the lists in place of the ousted Hasmoneans. Pockets of resistance still existed throughout the country. We know that one of these bases of Herod's enemy was under the command of a sister of Antigonus. Even after the suppression of this desperate resistance, rebellion smouldered under the surface, so that Herod found it necessary to billet Roman troops near Jerusalem. Then came the battle of Actium, and its outcome seemed to seal Herod's fate. In this decisive hour of his political career Herod showed his complete unscrupulousness and also his great diplomatic adroitness. When he heard of Antony's defeat, he coolly dropped his defeated patron and took steps straightway to join the winning side. Before going to Rhodes, where Octavian had commanded him to appear and account for his friendship with Antony, he took the precaution of getting rid of the old high priest Hyrcanus whom he had lured back to Judea from his imprisonment in Parthia after the capture of Jerusalem. Contrary to all expectation, the interview with Octavian turned out extremely well for Herod. Herod managed not only to secure pardon for his failings but even to come out of the crisis with a significant territorial gain, for apart from his own territory valuable pieces of Cleopatra's territory were restored to him—Jericho, for example, with its balsam plantations—which had been taken from him by Antony at the queen's prompting. Herod now appeared even to his most bitter enemies to be undisputed master of Judea whom no one could any longer harm. For he was under the protection of the man at whose feet, since Actium, the world now lay.

Outwardly, therefore, Herod seemed to have won peace and security. But things were different inside his kingdom. One cause of the dissension surrounding Herod was the domestic trouble which clouded the king's life. Herod was of Idumean–Nabatean stock. Although the family had been forced to embrace Judaism some three generations before the events we are talking of, they were regarded, by their political opponents at least, as a clan of "half Jews". The proud Hasmoneans particularly turned up their noses at Herod and his family and called them "Hasmonean slaves". In the eyes of these aristocrats the Antipaters were inferior upstarts and usurpers. Especially wounding to the king was the contempt shown him by his beloved Hasmonean wife. To this contempt was added a profound hatred when, for reasons of state, Herod had the queen's brother murdered, the sixteen-year-old high priest Aristobulus, and then her aged grandfather Hyrcanus. This made the break between the couple inevitable, and the fate of the queen was tragically and relentlessly acted out. Mariamne was subjected to a long and violent persecution behind which was the king's malicious sister, Salome, and then was condemned to death and executed. Her own violent death was very soon followed by those of her mother Alexandra and the entire, numerous male issue of the Hasmonean house.

This angry violence of the tyrant greatly embittered the people of Judea and intensified the hatred they felt for him. Herod reacted to this with pitiless severity. Secret police infiltrated everywhere and sought out enemies of the regime throughout the whole country. Suspects were arrested and taken to such fortresses as Hyrcania where they disappeared for ever, so that, as a later source reports, not even the bones of the victims could be discovered. Even so, it appears that opposition among the people was not entirely stamped out. For the famous law of Herod against "housebreakers" was in fact a counter-measure against the growing acts of terrorism by individuals, which were obviously directed against the tyrant as much as against his supporters—for such there were—in the country. In the language of the Roman conqueror, these "lone rangers" were called thieves and robbers. It is more true to see in them the precursors of the later Zealots and Sicarii.

Another reason why Herod's rule was so hated was that in general he was inclined to favour things Roman. Herod is supposed to have once said (the saying is recorded by Flavius Josephus) that he had more sympathy for the Greeks than for the Jews. If the words are an invention, they are a good invention. In actual fact, Herod's kingdom with his administrative apparatus, his strictly organized civil service, his carefully structured court, was completely styled on the pattern of Hellenistic states. It is true that the Hasmoneans, and Alexander Jannaeus in particular, had already begun "modernizing" their state in a Hellenistic direction. But Herod was the first to give real impetus to this development. Administration, the judiciary, taxation, tolls and harbour-dues, trade and commerce, all received special attention from the king, who had outstanding gifts of organization. There can be no doubt that general prosperity was greatly increased in this way, although it is undeniable that in Herod's state, as in every Hellenistic state, the burdens which the people had to carry were hard enough. But what completely outweighed all possible advantages in the eyes of the Jewish people was the fact that the king's activities were frequently coupled with a gross disregard for the law of the Torah. A blatant example of how Herod violated the law is the decree against "housebreakers", for not only was this a gross infringement of an explicit commandment in the Torah but, even more, it handed fellow Jewish citizens over to Gentiles so that they were lost to the faith of their fathers.

If this disregard of the Jewish law was calculated to arouse the indignation of the people, the founding of new cities, if anything, provoked their feelings even more, for these cities not only afforded military bases for controlling their country, but also created centres of Hellenistic, Gentile culture from where the "uncleanness of the nations" could be freely disseminated. Herod's policy of settling Gentile veterans who were hostile to Jews had in fact disastrous consequences, as became evident from events immediately after his death, and still more in the period of the procurators in Judea.

Herod's foundations became in time centres of fierce hatred against the Jews, which even penetrated the ranks of the Roman provincial administration and so prepared the ground for the tragic conflict between the Jewish nation and the Roman empire. Striking confirmation that this contention is right is given by the role which the city of Caesarea, the most important of Herod's foundations, played in these terrible events. It was this city which provided the occasion for the outbreak of the great war. As the rabbis put it, Jerusalem and Caesarea cannot exist at the same time; the existence of the one city implies the downfall of the other.

Another source of this widespread resentment was the gifts and donations made by the king to Gentile cities throughout the Hellenistic east and to the men of influence in Rome. Josephus has some remarkable things to say about the extent of these gifts. Herod believed he had to do this because he was all the time aware of the fact that he was a client-king who owed all his kingly authority to an act of grace on the part of the ruling power, Rome, and on the part of his august emperor. He had to do everything that the empire considered desirable. It was this disposition of Herod's in favour of things Roman which moved him to incorporate his own kingdom organically into the great imperial structure of Augustus, contrary to the separatist tendencies of the Jewish people, in order that it might share in the blessings of the new age inaugurated by the emperor, the blessings of the new Saeculum. Herod, in fact, wanted to be on a small scale in Judea what Augustus was on a large scale in the Roman empire—a benefactor and saviour.

This effort to emulate Augustus even extended to the reverence which the provinces of the Roman empire paid to Augustus as the saviour of the world; that is, it went as far as deification and ruler worship. Herod too demanded his statues and temples, as Josephus explicitly tells us. We have one piece of evidence, even though it is not quite conclusive, that there was a cult of Herod in Si'a in Trans-Jordan. Evidently a cult of Herod was possible only in the Gentile part of the kingdom. Even a Herod dare not institute in the Jewish part a cult which in the eyes of his Jewish subjects would inevitably be regarded as blatant paganism and idolatry. But Herod was not the man to forgo an honour which carried with it an important political element. If deification and ruler worship in their Gentile shape were impracticable in Judea, then something had to take their place which, while not according the king the divine worship which the emperor enjoyed, was even so suited somehow to raising him above the level of ordinary mortals and gave him a superhuman halo. This "something" was met by his taking on the role of herald of Roman imperial salvation in Judea. But he did this not by propagating Roman thinking pure and simple (as we frequently meet in inscriptions from the Hellenistic, eastern part of the empire as well as in Augustan literature, for instance, in Vergil and Horace) but rather by amalgamating the ideology of Rome with the ideology of Jewish messianism in such a way that the core was Roman and the dressing was Jewish messianic. At the centre of this Herodian concept of messianism stood Herod as the son of David for, since the saviour had to be of David's line, the king's ancestry was tailored (in accordance with ancient practice) to give it a Davidic origin. The Jewish people were to receive from his hand their share of the blessings of the new Roman Augustan Saeculum as an actualization of the messianic idea proclaimed by the Old Testament prophets.

This conception which we have sketched here only briefly was intended to furnish the Herodian regime with the legitimacy which it lacked in terms of Jewish religion. There is no doubt that it represented an unprecedented challenge to the national religious hopes of the Jewish people. It was in fact duly rejected by the Pharisaic opposition as well as by the political nationalists. The Pharisees were in no doubt that the Herodian regime was simply Gentile rule in another guise. They reasoned like this: Israel can receive salvation neither directly nor indirectly from the Gentiles but solely from God. It will come by the hand of his chosen one of the house of David as a reward for the presence of piety and upright living. This chosen one will come to redeem his people Israel at a time fixed by God at the beginning of creation. For these reasons Herod the bloody executioner of countless Jews and of his own family, Herod the tyrant who oppressed the people of Judea with brutal force, the lackey of the "impious regime" of Rome, cannot be the chosen one of God, nor can his reign be regarded as the coming reign of the chosen one. The Herodian kingdom is really an offshoot of the Gentile kingdom and will founder with it, in order to clear the way for the reign of the truly chosen one in the hour which God has determined in his inscrutable decree at the beginning of creation. Until then, Israel has the duty to have faith and wait.

This point of view was not, however, shared by the nationalist wing of the opposition to Herod in the country. They took exactly the same position as the Pharisees with regard to the messianic expectation as such, for they too hoped for the coming of the son of David according to God's decree. But they differed from the Pharisees in refusing to tolerate patiently the rule of the Romans and of their puppet Herod, calling instead for active opposition. At the beginning of Herod's reign this group gathered recruits from the ranks of the Hasmonean party in the widest sense of the word. After the Hasmoneans had been exterminated and their party destroyed, opposition under Herod's tyrannical rule could find vent only in terrorist acts carried out by individual fighters, against whom Herod brought in his law against "housebreakers", mentioned already.

This is how things stood in Judea as long as Herod was on the throne. But immediately after his death in 4 B.C., the storm broke in the country. Herod had provided in his will that the kingdom should be divided among his sons, Archelaus, Herod Antipas, and Philip, and that Archelaus should inherit the title of king along with the supremacy, while Galilee and Perea were to go to Herod Antipas with the title of tetrarch and the Trans-Jordan regions of Gaulanitis, Trachonitis, and Batanea as well as the city of Paneas to Philip, also with the title of tetrarch. The provision regarding Archelaus was not ratified by Augustus in its entirety. Instead of the title of king he received merely the title of ethnarch and the regions of Judea and Samaria. But the appointment turned out to be a mistake. Archelaus had inherited only the negative, not the positive, sides of his father. His handling of the agitated masses immediately after Herod's death was both perverse and cruel. By his actions Archelaus furthered the plans of the revolutionaries so that for the first time they had opportunity to become active on a large scale. Only the intervention of the governor of Syria, Quintilius Varus, put an end to general insurrection, but with terrible bloodshed. After ruling for ten years (4 B.C.–A.D. 6), Archelaus was deposed by order of Augustus and banished to Gaul. His territory was brought under an imperial procurator with military powers, who however was responsible to the governor of Syria. The same fate also befell Herod Antipas after a long reign (4 B.C.–A.D. 39). Only Philip, the mildest of the three heirs of Herod's patrimony, had a peaceful end (4 B.C.–A.D. 34). The object of putting Archelaus' territory under the direct control of a Roman provincial official was to keep the unsettled country in check and damp down the swelling rebellion. But the move turned out to be a mistake. For the procurators were for the most part brutal and incompetent and on the whole had no appreciation of the distinctiveness of the people entrusted to them.

So it came about that the ferment in the land, instead of diminishing, grew greater and greater. Sedition among the masses assumed more threatening proportions. The Roman provincial authorities had only one weapon against this activity of the revolutionaries—the use of violence. But this was a foolish policy, bound in the end to lead to catastrophe. The Roman administration never made even the slightest attempt to find a constructive solution to the problems of Judea. A solution might perhaps have been found if greater consideration had been given to the local situation than to the regular routine of Roman provincial government in the east. The peaceful episode of the reign of Agrippa I showed that there was a possibility of securing peace in the country despite all difficulties. Even the situation in relation to the parties in Judea was not so hopeless that serious efforts by the Romans to find a *modus vivendi* could not have found a positive response among considerable sections of the population. Of the four parties in Judea which Josephus lists—leaving aside the Sadducees, who just because of their class interests were unconditionally in favour of peace and quiet—even the vast majority of Pharisees were opposed to messianic militancy. The Essenes too appear to have been men of peace. Criticisms made against this view in recent years do not stand up to scrutiny. The men of the "fourth philosophy", as the Zealots were called by Josephus, the champions of a militant messianism, were originally a minority which a reasonable Roman policy in Judea could have held in check. The tragedy of the country was that the Pharisees, who exercised great influence over the people, remained virtually ignored as a political factor in Roman administrative circles. The Roman procurators were almost exclusively concerned with the struggle against the active extremists, and it was precisely this fact which helped the men of the "fourth philosophy", which goes back to A.D. 6, to become more and more popular. A wise Roman policy in Judea would have made use of the positive lessons of the period when Agrippa was king. Instead of this, it reverted after his death in A.D. 44 to the routine of direct provincial government, although it must have been clear to anyone with insight that this system of administration had been proved wrong in Judea. Even the rule of Agrippa II, the last ruling descendant of Herod the Great, would have been preferable to the maladministration of the procurators in Judea.

So catastrophe was unavoidable. Jerusalem perished because the Jews were unable to offer a realistic objective for the messianic hopes which had been fanned into flame, and could not reconcile themselves to the inevitability of Roman rule. It also perished because the Roman authorities were remarkably incapable of appreciating the distinctiveness of the Jewish people, a distinctiveness which made it impossible for them to submit without resistance to the yoke of the Roman conqueror, as all other subjugated peoples had done. "Augebat iras quod soli Judaei non cessissent", says Tacitus in the *Histories (v.10)*: it increased the resentment of the Roman that the Jews alone had refused to surrender. A timely recognition of what lay behind this distinctive stubbornness could perhaps have opened up a *modus vivendi* and averted the catastrophe of A.D. 70.

6 Sadducees and Pharisees

PAUL WINTER

At the time of Jesus the Jews formed a national community which was to a large extent resident in its own land, the land of Israel. The social structure of the Jewish people comprised all classes—rulers and subjects, priests and laity, rich and poor, educated and ignorant, wealthy landowners, bourgeoisie, craftsmen, labourers, farmers, free men, and slaves. This stratified character of the population of Judea resulted in a diversity of interests among the inhabitants, both social and religious. Social differences were reflected in political and religious attitudes. In the Jewish community of the day there were large numbers of societies and associations, unions and guilds, parties and sects, or whatever we want to call these groupings. It is rather misleading to use within Judaism refined terms drawn from the party structure of Christianity or of European politics. For one way in which the distinctive character of Judaism is expressed is that its organizations do not centre around purely religious or political foci; when associations spring up they do not come together like our "parties" for entirely political and economic reasons, nor are they differentiated from one another on purely religious lines, as is the case with "sects". In Judaism politics are never completely separate from religion, and religion is never divorced from politics. Both elements make up an indivisible whole. Only with this qualification can such words as "party" or "sect" be used of groupings within the Jewish community.

The most influential groups in Judea at the time of Jesus were those of the Sadducees and Pharisees. The historian Josephus gives us detailed information about both of them, and we also have literary material which we can say with a fair degree of certainty exhibits Sadducean or Pharisaic traits. Josephus himself was a Jew

and had grown up in Palestine. The writings of his which have survived are written in Greek and for Greeks, or at least for people
who were versed in Greek thought. The effect of this on his account
of the Jewish parties has its advantages for us as well as its dis-
advantages. In order to make himself comprehensible to his readers,
Josephus expressed himself in Greek concepts and was particularly
at pains to present the party groupings of the people with intellectual precision and conceptual clarity. A Jewish writer writing for
Jews would never have gone to such lengths to contrast the beliefs
of the Pharisees and Sadducees almost systematically. In this respect
it is to our advantage that Josephus was conscious of having Greeks,
and Romans of Greek education, as readers. On the other hand, it is
precisely this clear-cut distinction between their beliefs which creates
a certain disadvantage. For there is a danger that we may overrate
the significance which doctrinal criteria had for these parties. Doctrinal definitions have played a great part in the history of Christianity. This is not the case in Judaism. Sadducees and Pharisees
may have wrangled with one another and they may have opposed
one another; but they did not excommunicate one another because
of differences of belief. When they were at odds, it was not because
they disagreed over the resurrection of the dead, but because they
differed over practical questions relating to the cult or to the
observance of the law.

The older of the two "sects" were the Sadducees. They were not
really a doctrinal party, for their beliefs were identical with those of
the Hebrew Bible, the law and the prophets. As to their origins we
can only make conjectures. Perhaps Ezekiel should be regarded as
being already one of the spiritual fathers of the Sadducees, for he
particularly emphasized that the office of priest was the prerogative
of the house of Zadok. If it is true that the name "Sadducee" is
derived from the name of Zadok, the priest of Solomon's day, the
Sadducean party would be of very early origin, even if it did not
constitute a party grouping until after the Exile. We cannot tell
whether Ezra or Nehemiah had "Sadducean" tendencies, for we
know too little about the parties of their day. It could be that the
preferential treatment of priests which both Ezra and Nehemiah
made a particular concern of theirs was connected with the group
which later came to be called Sadducee. We have no historical
records in which the word "Sadducee" is used to describe a party
until the middle of the second century B.C. By then the Sadducees

had already passed their spiritual heyday, although the party as such still enjoyed a powerful position among the Jewish people. The spiritual high-water mark for Sadduceeism was reached around the turn of the third and second centuries B.C. Probably we can see a Sadducee in the author of the book of "The Preacher" (Ecclesiastes). Certainly the authors of the "Book of the Wisdom of Jesus, the Son of Sirach" (Ecclesiasticus) and of the First Book of Maccabees can be identified as Sadducees.

These few considerations are enough to show that there were different currents or trends even within the Sadducean party. In "The Preacher" there is worldly wisdom and resignation which verges on cynicism, in Ben Sirach sober down-to-earth wisdom side by side with religious mysticism, in Maccabees the enthusiasm of political freedom. As we know from Josephus, the Sadducees were averse to innovations, particularly in matters of cult or law. They recognized the written law as binding. Their attitude towards oral traditions was reserved. This must not be taken to mean that the Sadducees had no oral tradition at all. Without explanations handed down orally, legal maxims within the Torah in apodictic form ("Thou shalt not") could not have been enforced. The Sadducees, who were devoted to the strict fulfilment of the law, could not therefore have managed without auxiliary ordinances. But they did not allow that regulations which had been handed down only orally had any absolute authority. Wherever possible they interpreted the law literally, differing here from the Pharisees who showed greater flexibility in matters of the law. Josephus says that the Sadducees denied the immortality of the soul and did not believe in the reward of good deeds and the punishment of bad deeds after death. The immortality of the soul is Josephus' way of putting the doctrine of the resurrection in the language of Greek thought. The Sadducees believed neither in the resurrection of the dead nor in angelic beings or spirits nor in predestination. Their thinking was realistically sober.

For a real understanding of the Sadducees we need to consider their social background. They were the party of the rich, of the chief priests, the landed nobility, the party of the property owners. As such they were generally conservative in outlook, averse to any sort of innovation. To preserve their property and influence they pursued a policy of accommodation towards foreign powers. But it would be wrong on this account to say that they had no national

sympathies and to label the Sadducees simply as the "party of
collaborators". There were times when it was the Sadducees who
kept the national flag flying while others were prepared to compromise with foreign powers. Along with their class interests the
Sadducees had a concern for the preservation of old traditions and
national institutions. In the second century and at the beginning of
the first century B.C., the Sadducees were still the most influential
political force among the Jewish people. The many internal rifts and
frequent wars with foreign powers bore especially hard on the
classes from which the Sadducees were mostly drawn. The party
waned in significance, first spiritually and later politically too. Even
so until A.D. 70 the Sadducees provided the men on whom the
highest offices of Jewish internal government devolved—the high
priests and their advisers, the majority of the members of the
supreme council, the commanders of the Temple guard, the
treasurers and other functionaries of the community. In their
dealings with foreign powers, with the Romans for instance, they
had to act on behalf of a people who watched them with distrust
and gave them little support. When the Jewish revolt broke out
against Rome, the heads of the leading Sadducees were among the
first to fall victim to the people's anger.

The Pharisees can more justly be regarded as a doctrinal party
than the Sadducees. In their case too the social background must not
be ignored, but their emphasis on religious thinking and conduct
comes much more to the fore. The name "Pharisee" comes from the
Hebrew word *perush*. They called themselves "the separated ones",
that is those who kept away from any who were ritually unclean.
The origin of their name in itself gives an indication how they
differed from the Sadducees. For the Sadducees apparently derived
their name from a dignitary of the past, and so emphasized that they
belonged to a privileged class by birth, whereas the Pharisees, by
calling themselves "the separated ones", had a name which put the
stress on the act of making a voluntary, individual decision. The
Pharisees originally came from the class of craftsmen. By their own
choice and inclination they devoted themselves to the study of the
Torah, earning their living in various jobs which were usually
poorly paid. These groups then produced scholars who were listened
to and respected by the people because of their learning and not
(like the priests) because of their birth. The priests had their centre
in the Temple at Jerusalem; the leaders of the Pharisees, later called

rabbis, taught in the synagogues and combined to found houses of learning. The rise in social status of the Pharisees brought about a relaxation in their initially rigorous separation from society. Even before the destruction of the Temple, men of priestly descent joined the Pharisees from time to time.

We are told by Josephus that by the middle of the second century B.C. the Pharisees could be distinguished from other groups by their particular tenets. Very probably they were then a relatively new party. They were helped on at first by the Hasmoneans when this served Hasmonean interests, for the Hasmoneans were able to make only slow headway against the old priestly nobility. But later the Pharisees found themselves in opposition to the established priest-princes, in particular to John Hyrcanus and Alexander Jannaeus. When the latter's widow came to the throne at his death, the Pharisees again acquired influence. In the struggle between the sons of Alexander, they supported the older brother, the weak-willed John Hyrcanus II, against his energetic younger brother, Aristobulus. Under Herod the Pharisees lost their influence in the affairs of government but considerably increased their following. At the time of Jesus they and their supporters were the biggest grouping of Jews in the country but politically not the most influential. They formed a minority in the supreme council. In the New Testament scribes are often mentioned in conjunction with the Pharisees. The two must not be confused. "Scribe", which means a legal expert, was the title of an office and belonged to those who were versed in the law of the land. In the Jewish state the Torah, the law of God, was the basic law of the community, so scribes as well as Pharisees applied themselves to the study of the Torah, the former in order to further their professional interests, the latter for the sake of knowledge itself. As the general prestige of the Pharisees increased, the number of scribes who were sympathetic to Pharisaism also increased. But there were still scribes who were not Pharisees. In the Gospels the Pharisees are represented as the most bitter opponents of Jesus. This is a biased view. The disciples of Jesus tried to win a hearing, and looked for likely converts among the same classes as those from which the followers of the Pharisees were drawn. From the point of view of the history of religion, Jesus himself was much closer to the Pharisees than to any other sect of the time. As the example of Paul shows, Pharisees were the easiest to win over to Jesus. There was little point in arguing with the Sadducees, for they were too far removed from the circle of Jesus' disciples to be won over as followers.

The separateness of the Pharisees should not be taken as meaning that they were unaffected by influences from outside Judea. Judea was a transit country where movements from surrounding countries converged. Neither the Sadducees nor the Pharisees could completely protect themselves against religious influences from outside Judaism. During the Exile in Babylon and still more under Persian rule and in the period of the Diadochi, ideas which were not Jewish in origin came to be accepted among large sections of the Jewish people. In view of the geographical position of the country and the close contacts maintained with Jews of the dispersion, this was only to be expected. To use a catchphrase, we could say that the Sadducees were more "western", that is, they were more open to the rational, Greek way of thinking, than to eastern influences from Babylon and Iran. The Pharisees on the other hand were more "eastern". Ideas which bore the marks of Babylonian and Persian origin, such as speculations about angels, astral spirits, and demons, as well as the belief in resurrection, penetrated the lower classes of the people more quickly than the educated and wealthy circles. If we look at the sweep of world history we see the same thing happening with the expansion of Christianity. The ancient aristocratic families of Rome held to the old religion, while the proletarian masses proved to be much less resistant to popular movements coming from the eastern Mediterranean basin.

We know very little about the Pharisees from the time of Jesus himself. For information about their attitudes and convictions we have to go back a few generations to Josephus' accounts of the early Hasmonean period and to the Psalms of Solomon, or to early rabbinic tradition several generations later. Josephus says: "The Pharisees teach that some things but not all are the immediate production of fate and that certain things are in our own power to do."[1] If we put this back into the language of Jewish ideas from its translation into Greek thought, it means that the Pharisees taught that what happens in the world stands under God's sway but the choice of deciding between good and evil rests with man. The Pharisees believed in the resurrection of the dead and in a judgement of the righteous and sinners; they believed in angels and spirits. The belief

---

[1] *Antiquities xiii. 9*

in the resurrection, which is foreign to the Old Testament (with the exception of one late passage), had been taken over from Persia and was developed in several stages by the Jews. At first they thought only of a resurrection of the righteous who in the next world would receive the reward denied them here. Later there developed the doctrine of the general resurrection of both the righteous and sinners, and this linked up with the idea of the judgement of the world at which eternal life was meted out to the former and damnation to the latter. It is wrong to think that the Pharisees as a body promised a share in the blessedness of the next world only to Israelites. "The righteous of all peoples share in the world to come" runs a frequently quoted saying of the rabbis. The Pharisees preached penitence and repentance of sin as the way of bringing in the kingdom of God. "When the Israelites do penance, they are redeemed." The Midrash says that God withdraws his presence from the world in times of human wickedness, but in times of recollection draws near again to the world. This conviction explains why the Pharisees made such efforts to obey God completely. Fulfilling the law was never for them a matter of external observance only. Even if they took great pains "to cleanse the outside of the cup and the plate", they did not do so to cover up inner uncleanness, but because they saw their vocation from God as the complete fulfilment of the law. If the accusation of a merely external observance misses the mark, so too does that of legalistic hair-splitting. Paul and Tarphon were separated by something like a generation. Both of them were Pharisees. The one became a Christian, the other an opponent of Christianity. Like Paul earlier, Tarphon was equally convinced that it is impossible to fulfil God's demands completely. But out of this realization he drew a different conclusion from Paul's. One of the few sayings of his which have come down to us—a saying which is enough for us to see that Rabbi Tarphon was one of the great men of all time—runs: "It is not for you to complete the work, but neither is it for you to hold back from the work of completion." No less than St Paul, Rabbi Tarphon understood completely the tragic situation of man in relation to God. But unlike Paul, he did not look for a paradoxical way out of this situation.

Like Jesus, the Pharisees taught the coming of the kingdom of God. The idea of "the kingdom of God"—or more correctly "the universal reign of God"—is common to both primitive Christianity and Pharisaic, rabbinic Judaism. It was not part of the thinking of

5

the Sadducees, and so far has not turned up in the recently discovered writings of the desert community beside the Dead Sea. The
belief that the coming of God's reign depends on the conduct of
man is a sign of the active, unfatalistic strain of Pharisaism. Without
prejudice to God's sovereignty man has a part to play in bringing in
the kingdom. In connection with this belief one other about the idea
of rewards, as it is called, may also be mentioned. The doctrine of
recompensing good and bad deeds, which also occurs in the preaching of Jesus, was undoubtedly current among the Pharisees too.
Although this doctrine is found in Jesus' preaching, some Christian
theologians have not been able to resist reproaching the rabbis of the
Pharisees with having very narrow minds and have asserted that the
Jew reckons up with God how much God owes him for the fulfilment of his commandments. Such a caricature bears no relation to
the truth. When Rabbi Meir was brought the news that his friend
and teacher Elisha ben Abuyah had renounced Judaism, Rabbi Meir
said nothing for a little while and then remarked:

> How blessed is Elisha ben Abuyah. His action can never be forgiven,
> neither in this world nor in the next. He is one of the few men who
> are free to do good without being able to expect a reward.

So far we have mentioned the differences between the beliefs of
the Sadducees and Pharisees over the existence of angels, the resurrection of the dead, the Last Judgement, and retribution after death.
We have said nothing of what either believed about the eschatological messiah. Josephus tells us nothing about the subject. Whether
he was silent because it seemed to him undesirable to discuss this
subject openly for Gentile readers or because at the time to which
his account of the Jewish parties applies there was still no developed
ideology about the messiah, is a question which need not now be
discussed. In any case the word "messiah" underwent a considerable
change of meaning in the course of Jewish history. It is used in the
Old Testament of the ruler of the day—the king or high priest.
Then, when the Jewish people came under foreign rule, it became
the designation of the one they expected to liberate them from the
Gentiles. Among the Essenes it seems that the hope that a messiah
would come had already arisen by the beginning of the Maccabean
wars. They longed for a priest from the line of Zadok, whose task
they believed it was to lead the people. It is open to question whether
by the early Hasmonean period other groups also looked for the

coming of a messiah. In the late Hasmonean and post-Hasmonean period this belief did win acceptance among the Pharisees too, and reached its most beautiful liturgical expression in the Psalms of Solomon. As for the Sadducees, it is improbable that they ever shared the belief in an eschatological messiah. We cannot say with absolute certainty whether this is true or not, because our sources are silent about it. But their traditional interpretation of scripture alone would hardly have suggested to the Sadducees any belief in a messiah like that held by the community of Jesus or by the Pharisees. Moreover, they were anxious to work peacefully and without friction with the Ptolemies, Seleucids, and later the Romans; political caution would have ruled out for them any fervent and enthusiastic expectation of a messiah in the eschatological sense of the word. For them the word still had the old, temporal sense as in the Old Testament and was the title of the reigning high priest. So the question "Are you the messiah, the son of the most high?" is quite impossible on the lips of a Sadducean high priest, for the high priest laid claim to the title of messiah for himself.

In contrast to the Sadducees, the Pharisees considered matters of state politics to be of only subordinate importance. They were concerned more with preserving their doctrines in their purity than with the political independence of the nation. Thus, after A.D. 70, the Pharisees were able to come to terms with Roman rule more easily than did other Jewish parties or groupings. They looked for the redemption of Israel and the world, not by an expansion of political power, but by unconditional observance of the commandments. In order to entreat God's mercy on this people, they endeavoured to make their daily lives pleasing to God. It is due to the Pharisees that after the military defeat in A.D. 70, when the Temple fell and the autonomy of the nation came to an end, the distinctive character of the Jewish people remained intact, even if this was achieved at the price of some spiritual narrowing and of the surrender of all national claims to power and the abandonment of all apocalyptically tinged hopes.

As we said at the beginning, definitions of religious doctrine do not have the same importance in Judaism as they do in the history of Christianity. What is important in Judaism, in all sects and parties, is the belief in one God, creator of the world and lord of history. For the rest, there is great freedom. Whether a Jew believes in a life after death or not, whether he believes in angels and spirits or not, whether he is looking for a messiah or not, does not make him a Jew and does not exclude him from Judaism. It was characteristic of the relationship of the Sadducees and Pharisees that although they were often at odds with one another, they did not quarrel over differences of belief. They disputed about cultic regulations, the form of sacrificial worship, how to fix the calendar of feasts and the like, that is, about matters of practice, but not about doctrinal definitions. "It is not discussion that is important but action", as one of the "Sayings of the Fathers" has it. A Jew expresses his belief not in confessions but in deeds.

7 Apocalyptic and Eschatology

KLAUS KOCH

In any scholarly inquiry into the origins of Christianity the question inevitably arises which religious and spiritual traditions made their impress on Jesus, his disciples, and early Christianity. It is not easy for the historian to give an answer, for at the end of the first century B.C. the people of Israel were not a spiritual unity. The different religious-cum-political parties in Palestine at that time, such as the Pharisees, Sadducees, Essenes, Zealots, and Herodians, were at loggerheads with one another. The apocalyptic movement was one such grouping, a movement which is both interesting and mysterious, unusually fertile in producing literature, but difficult to relate historically to the contemporary history of Palestine. For this reason scholarship in the last sixty years has bypassed this thorny area. But with apocalyptic writings appearing among the sensational finds of scrolls by the Dead Sea, scholarly interest in this late Israelite movement is again beginning to be aroused in some measure. Impetus has also been given to the more recent studies of apocalyptic by the theory which Ernst Käsemann put forward five years ago. According to Käsemann apocalyptic is "the mother of all Christian theology". This thesis has provoked opposition, not least from Käsemann's former teacher, Rudolf Bultmann. It is still being hotly contested among biblical scholars.

Disputes about the value of apocalyptic ideas are nothing new to Christian theology. They have kept on flaring up from time to time in the history of the Church. For instance, Søren Kierkegaard expressed the harsh view a century ago that the true believer is closest of all to God, "while an apocalyptist is the furthest removed from him". That is, he pilloried apocalyptic as the worst perversion in theology. And five hundred years ago the reformer Martin Luther passed a violently ironic judgement on the Second Book of Esdras, the only apocalyptic writing then known from the Old Testament and Apocrypha apart from the Book of Daniel: "Fling the dreamer into the Elbe." On the other hand, there have always been outsiders who have particularly made the apocalyptic books of the Bible the centre of their theological systems. They include such men as the famous scientist Isaac Newton.

Before I go into the characteristic ideas of these books, let me briefly mention which are the most important apocalypses. In the New Testament there is one book of apocalyptic, the Revelation of John—a reminder that apocalyptic played a part in primitive Christianity too. In so far as I shall be dealing with the pre-Christian period in what follows, I shall confine myself to apocalyptic of Old Testament times. First in this category is the Book of Daniel. In its first part it tells of the fate of the young Israelite nobleman Daniel, who with three friends is carried off to Babylon at the fall of Jerusalem and there at the court of king Nebuchadnezzar quickly rises to office, although—or rather because—he resists all temptations to renounce his monotheistic faith. The legends of the three men in the fiery furnace, of the writing on the palace wall, and of Daniel in the lions' den, have made a deep impression on readers of all periods. But in the context of the whole book these stories are only introductions to the second part, which tells of four visions that came to Daniel in the night. In them is disclosed how and why a period of foreign empires must follow after the period of Israelite independence and how then after five hundred years through the appearing of a "Son of man" this foreign dominion is to be replaced by the everlasting kingdom of God. The Book of Daniel was written during the revolt of the Maccabees, 167–164 B.C., and reflects the turmoil of those years when the practice of the Israelite religion was prohibited on pain of death and the continuance of Israel put in jeopardy as never before. Out of this situation emerged an imminent eschatological expectation, a passionate hope that the kingdom of God was to be established on earth in the immediate future. This was the beginning of the apocalyptic movement, and the Book of Daniel is the oldest witness to it.

Next must be mentioned the First Book of Enoch, also called Ethiopic Enoch, because it is preserved in its entirety only in the Ethiopian Bible. It represents a collection of several separate apocalypses of the second and first centuries B.C. They are put into the mouth of the patriarch Enoch, who according to Genesis was the seventh man after Adam, and of whom Genesis says that "Enoch walked with God; and he was not, for God took him". The Book of Enoch tells how this Enoch was taken on a remarkable journey across the whole earth, through the underworld, and through the heavens, and thus saw how in the celestial regions all preparations had been made for the end of the world. Another rich source for apocalyptic ideas is the Second Book of Baruch or the Syriac Apocalypse of Baruch, preserved intact only in a single Syriac manuscript. The historical Baruch was a friend and secretary of the prophet Jeremiah about 600 B.C. In the Apocalypse, which was written perhaps at the end of the first century B.C., peculiar experiences and visions are ascribed to him during the fall and destruction of the city of Jerusalem. In them the mission of the chosen people is presented with regard to all the nations. Lastly, we have the Second Book of Esdras, an apocalypse which has not only come down in many eastern languages but is also included in the Latin version of the official Roman Catholic Bible. This book, which Luther would have preferred to send for ever to the bottom of the Elbe, is without doubt the most intellectually profound of the Jewish apocalypses, as well as the latest. It dates from about A.D. 100. As with Daniel and Second Baruch, the contents are backdated to the sixth century B.C., to the time of the Babylonian Exile and so to the darkest hour of Jewish history.

All the apocalypses have a fictitious author, that is they are, to use the technical term, "pseudepigrapha". They claim to be written by a famous person in ancient Israel, while in fact they were composed by anonymous scholars around the end of the first century B.C. Are they not then worthless forgeries? This indeed is how they were regarded for a long time by biblical scholars. Today, however, we are beginning to realize that the modern idea of literary originality is not appropriate to this literature. In their visions and auditory experiences the anonymous apocalyptists feel themselves to be identified in a mysterious way with the men of earlier times whose names they take. They regard themselves as "extensions of personality" of Daniel, Enoch, Baruch, or Ezra. It would be completely inappropriate to attribute deceitful motives to them.

These apocalyptic writings soon fell into oblivion. They have only come to light again through the manuscript discoveries of the last century. Why did they disappear? The fervent eschatological

expectation of apocalyptic was too abnormal for Judaism and the
strong emphasis on the figure of a saviour who was to come smacked
too much of Christianity. So the rabbis discarded the books. Rabbi
Akiba, who lived around A.D. 100, even made the remark that anyone merely taking these books·in his hand would forfeit salvation.
Christianity in the post-New-Testament period soon turned towards
Hellenistic metaphysics and so to a quite different way of thinking.
Because of this the symbolic, oriental thought-patterns of apocalyptic
and its cryptic, eschatological discourses became increasingly incomprehensible. So the early Fathers of the Church soon put out of
court a type of literature which at one time had been of prime
importance for Jesus and the first Christians.

What is the distinctive nature of apocalyptic? The Greek word
apokalypsis means a disclosure, an unveiling. An apocalypse then is
a work which discloses the secrets behind the course of the universe.
This is not done with scholarly reserve or with philosophical detach-
ment. The authors, the apocalyptists, are personally involved. They
are convinced that the end of the world is immediately at hand, and
so they look with longing for the Day of Judgement. Everything
they write is attributed by them to direct divine inspiration which
comes to them through visions and auditory experiences after long
struggle in prayer and fasting. If this does bring an experience of
divine illumination, the apocalyptists are cut to the quick, fall to the
ground, tremble all over, or for a long time lie motionless. What
they then write down is addressed to the wise and inspired among
men and claims to appear to the initiate as both logical and necessary. It is of course difficult for the modern reader to agree with this
claim. The enigmatic language of apocalyptic, with its mythical
imagery which is so difficult to interpret and its abstruse speculations in astronomy and cosmology, is more likely to make us shake
our heads and ridicule it. It is easy to see why rabbinic Judaism and
most Christian bodies have eliminated apocalyptic literature from
their Old Testament. But this is only one side of the case. It must
not be ignored on the other side that the apocalyptists succeeded in
sketching for the first time a coherent eschatology, a doctrine of the
end of the world and its restoration. The aphoristic predictions of
the prophets about the future of Israel, the destruction of the
Temple and of the Jewish state, as well as those about the establish-
ment of a new covenant and the coming of a messiah, are arranged
systematically and applied not just to the narrow sphere of the one

chosen people but to all the nations of the world. And so they talk of the coming kingdom of God which one day will break in on earth out of the world beyond, bringing with it a complete transformation of human society, so that oppression, sin, and pain will disappear for ever from the face of the earth. This state of everlasting righteousness will be brought about by a figure who will become the centre of restored humanity. He is occasionally called the messiah, but more usually "the Son of man". As soon as the Son of man appears, there will be a resurrection of the dead, so that the generations long dead can also share in the new world. Hope in a resurrection was previously unknown in Israel. In the Old Testament it is mentioned only in apocalyptic writings. In the New Testament, on the other hand, belief in a resurrection is an accepted assumption just like the ideas of the kingdom of God and the Son of man, which also originated in apocalyptic. So apocalyptic proves to be the bridge which binds together the Old and the New Testaments by means of eschatology and links up the prophets with the community of Jesus.

A good idea of what apocalyptic thinking is like is given by the seventh chapter of the Book of Daniel. In a vision the seer sees symbolic figures which illuminate for him the existence of the great world powers and the dramatic end of the present era.

Daniel said: "I saw in my vision by night, and behold, the four winds of heaven were stirring up the great sea. And four great beasts came up out of the sea, different from one another. The first was like a lion and had eagle's wings. Then as I looked its wings were plucked off, and it was lifted up from the ground and made to stand upon two feet like a man; and the mind of a man was given to it. And behold, another beast, a second one, like a bear. It was raised up on one side; it had three ribs in its mouth between its teeth; and it was told, 'Arise, devour much flesh.' After this I looked, and lo, another, like a leopard, with four wings of a bird on its back; and the beast had four heads; and dominion was given to it. After this I saw in the night visions, and behold, a fourth beast, terrible and dreadful and exceedingly strong; and it had great iron teeth; it devoured and broke in pieces, and stamped the residue with its feet. It was different from all the beasts that were before it" (7.2–7).

This is the first part of the vision. The symbolic language is characteristic of apocalyptic. Four weird beasts climb one after another out of the sea, the symbol of vast hordes of people. What are

these mythical creatures meant to be? There is an interpretation at
the end of the vision: "These four great beasts are four kingdoms
which shall arise out of the earth."

The vision deals, then, with four world powers of antiquity. The
first, the lion with eagle's wings, is the neo-Babylonian kingdom
which overthrew the small Israelite state of Jerusalem in 587 B.C.
The neo-Babylonian era is represented as a lion-cum-griffin, an
iconographic motif in Babylonian art. The other symbolic beasts too
are probably taken from the art of the country concerned and would
be immediately comprehensible to the initiate. The half-erect bear
is the next, representing the kingdom of the Medes, who at roughly
the same time as the Neo-Babylonians conquered the northern part
of the Near East. The three ribs in its mouth are no doubt three
previously independent countries. The third beast, the four-headed
leopard, stands for the empire of the Persians, who around 550 B.C.
overthrew the Neo-Babylonian and Median kings and won a world-
wide empire which stretched from Greece to India. Two hundred
years later the Persian empire was swept away by the kingdom of
Alexander the Great and his Hellenistic successors, who ruled the
eastern Mediterranean until replaced by the Romans shortly before
the end of the first century B.C. The Hellenistic period is symbolized
by the fourth beast, the dragon-like monster.

What purpose did the apocalyptist have in mind in symbolizing
the periods of history by means of peculiar creatures? His intention
was to portray the essential character of these periods, and at the
same time to make an interpretation of the course of the history of
the world. History is reduced to its root forces. The way the four
creatures appear one after another indicates a decline for the worse,
an increasing disintegration. Lion, then bear, then leopard, then
dragon: clearly a downward trend. So too the situation deteriorates
with the rule of the Neo-Babylonians, then the Medes, then the
Persians, and then the Hellenistic kings.

The author of Daniel understands the five hundred years prior to
him as an inevitable sequence of four world powers. From Daniel
on this idea becomes the keystone of the apocalyptists' understanding of history. But the fourth kingdom soon comes to be interpreted
as the Roman empire and no longer as the Hellenistic successors of
Alexander the Great. This transference to the Romans is found in
both 2 Esdras and 2 Baruch. And the New Testament apocalypse,
the Book of Revelation, follows this new tradition when in chapter 13

it depicts the Romans in the figure of the dragon-like monster. The apocalyptists' concept of the four monarchies then found its way into the western philosophy of history and was current there right until the eighteenth century.

The vision of the four kingdoms in Daniel 7 is followed by a completely different scene.

> As I looked, thrones were placed and one that was ancient of days took his seat; his raiment was white as snow, and the hair of his head like pure wool; his throne was fiery flames, its wheels were burning fire. A stream of fire issued and came forth from before him; a thousand thousands served him, and ten thousand times ten thousand stood before him; the court sat in judgment, and the books were opened.... And as I looked, the last beast was slain, and its body destroyed and given over to be burned with fire (7.9–11).

> I saw in the night visions, and behold, with the clouds of heaven there came one like a son of man, and he came to the Ancient of Days and was presented before him. And to him was given dominion and glory and kingdom, that all peoples, nations, and languages should serve him; his dominion is an everlasting dominion, which shall not pass away, and his kingdom one that shall not be destroyed (7.13–14).

The history of the world is heading for inevitable catastrophe. For this reason the ancient God takes his seat and begins the Last Judgement. The books of history are opened and the world powers partly destroyed, partly pardoned but degraded. Then a figure comes forward whose appearance, like that of God, can be described only allusively. He assumes the rule of the world but exercises his rule in a completely different way from that of the previous powerful tyrants. "A son of man", the author writes. In translation the phrase sounds as though it has a biological reference which the original text does not carry. The equivalent words in Hebrew and Aramaic have a much wider connotation than we understand by "son", and often mean simply the individual member of a group or the individual specimen of a genus. "Son of man" means nothing more than "the individual man" or, with emphasis, "the man *par excellence*", the individual in whom the essence of humanity comes to expression. That is what it means here. The Son of man who appears before the throne of heaven and is given dominion over all nations by the ancient God is, in Daniel's vision, the essentially human one, whose form of government cannot be compared with the bestial, or worse than bestial, conduct of his predecessors. Under his lordship the kingdom of God is realized and assumes a visible form here on earth; this is the eternal kingdom which will never pass away. The heavenly kingdom has already been in control behind the events of the world but in secret and only apparent to the eye of faith. Now, after the great judgement of the world, it is finally established on earth.

The role of the Son of man as the one who represents all humanity before the transcendent God has been thought out further in apocalyptic after Daniel. More and more functions are ascribed to him. He is seen not only as the eternal ruler in the coming kingdom of God but also soon as the one who institutes the great judgement of the world and sits upon the throne of God. The Book of Daniel still reserves for God alone the universal judgement, but by 1 Enoch it is attributed to the Son of man. Enoch hears the word of God: "On that day my elect one shall sit on the throne of glory and shall try the works of men." According to Enoch, in order that the Last Judgement can be carried out justly and impartially among all men, it is preceded by a general resurrection of all the dead which the Son of man also brings about.

Apocalyptic eschatology then came to be appropriated by primitive Christianity. There are sentences not only in the Revelation of John but also in the Gospels which could just as well have occurred in the apocalypses we have mentioned. For instance, in Matthew 25 we read:

> When the Son of man comes in his glory, and all the angels with him, then he will sit on his glorious throne. Before him will be gathered all the nations, and he will separate them one from another as a shepherd separates the sheep from the goats.

And the New Testament expects the resurrection of the dead to be brought about by Jesus, just as the apocalypses expect the Son of man to do. Alongside this there is another motif which runs through the New Testament which considers that the Son of man has already appeared in Jesus of Nazareth, and that the revision of all values has already begun in Jesus. Either way—whether primitive Christianity looks for the second coming of Christ and the final breaking-in of the kingdom of God, or whether it ardently acknowledges that the Son of man has already come—the theological structure is in both cases built up with materials from Old Testament apocalyptic.

It is not only the eschatology of apocalyptic that has left its legacy but also the scheme it presents of world history. According to apocalyptic thinking the point in time when the end of the world occurs is not just an arbitrary time, as though one day someone happens to put his finger on the button. Rather, the course of political and religious history runs demonstrably towards an end of the world and a revolutionary renewal of mankind. The apocalyptists believe that it is possible to observe the signs of the times and to fix the point in time when the measure of sin is full and God will intervene. The end of the existing situation and the termination of all power blocks is calculated, if not to the day and hour, then to the year or at least to the decade. On this point Jesus did not follow apocalyptic ideas. Jesus expressly refused to fix the date and hour of the end and did not concern himself with the epochs of world history. Even so, theologians and philosophers soon took up again the apocalyptic interpretation of history. For it was apocalyptic that attempted for the first time to go beyond the history of a particular nation to give a comprehensive view of the history of mankind. Basically all the ideologies of world history which have been devised since then, from Augustine to Hegel and Karl Marx, have borne the impress of this origin.

In the three centuries from 200 B.C. to A.D. 100, the apocalyptic movement was at its prime. Soon after that it experienced a violent rejection on the part of Jewish and Christian theologians. Even so they did not speak the last word on the intellectual status and the theological achievements of this literature. Time and again right up to the present day, theology and philosophy have found themselves having to decide what they make of the apocalyptic interpretation of history and eschatology. And indeed, a thesis is being put forward with all seriousness today that in historical fact Christian theology developed at first under the influence of apocalyptic. All this shows how extremely significant this extraordinary movement in late Judaism is, even though only fragments of its extensive writings have been preserved to us.

8 The Qumran Community

HERBERT BRAUN

Within the last twenty years our knowledge of the time of Jesus has been enlarged by a' very important and highly interesting area of study. In the spring of 1947 (or 1945?) a number of writings, previously unknown, were discovered in one of the numerous caves in the marly country at the north-west corner of the Dead Sea. It soon became apparent that they were the writings of a distinctive Jewish sect, which came to be given the name of the Qumran community after the place where the scrolls were found. Excavations and searches during the next few years brought to light the foundations of an entire organized settlement which had been the centre of this community from the second century B.C. until A.D. 68, apart from a gap of twenty-seven years. After 1947 further caves were discovered containing similar writings.

The scrolls that have been found are written mostly in Hebrew, less often in Aramaic, and occasionally in Greek. They include some texts of parts of the Old Testament. But for the most part they make up a literary corpus derived from the Qumran community. A few of them, such as the Damascus scroll and some which we class with Old Testament pseudepigrapha and apocrypha, were known to us before the Qumran discoveries. The majority of them, such as the most important of the scrolls—the Manual of Discipline, as it is called, in various versions and two supplements, the Qumran psalter, the War Scroll, the various expositions or commentaries on Old Testament books, of which the Commentary on Habakkuk is the best known—only came to light with this find twenty years ago and now add considerably to our knowledge of that Judaism contemporary with Jesus of Nazareth and the early Church.

We did already have some information about a sect of Essenes from Jewish writers of the first century A.D., and the Essenes have a considerable affinity with the Qumran community, even though particular groups of the Qumran community, which itself was not completely homogeneous, are not at all identical with the Essenes. However, our knowledge of these Essenes was based on Jewish accounts which were to a greater or less extent coloured by Hellenistic influences and merely told us *about* this sect. Now we have a really extensive corpus of writings—so extensive in fact that it has not yet all been published—which was composed inside the Qumran community itself or was handed down particularly by them. This corpus expresses in their own words and phrases what the Qumran community thought and believed. What sort of community was this? What did they believe and what views did they hold?

The Qumran community is to be seen as one of the eschatological sects outside the limits of conventional Judaism. The important thing for them is the observance of *all* the commandments in the light of a particularly rigorous interpretation of the law of Moses. You must cut yourself off from all who do not share this serious intent. If you take the step of joining the Qumran community, this includes the renunciation of official Judaism. For the world is governed by two powers or spirits. Light and darkness, faithfulness and wickedness, always have their adherents, their "sons", among men. So the members of this community, the sons of light, have to separate themselves very rigorously from the sons of darkness, for the struggle between the two powers goes on inexorably with now one, now the other uppermost, until God puts an end to the world. In fact this struggle also goes on in the hearts of the sons of light themselves, so fiercely do light and darkness contend with each other. This dualism cannot be regarded as absolute. God has created both sorts of spirit and he leads the cause of light to final victory. God determines every man's share in light and darkness. But this does not make man passive. Rather, he is called on to make the right decision for himself.

What sort of decision is this? It means being prepared to undertake complete obedience to the law by entering this community. The member of Qumran owes love and faithfulness to his brethren within the community. But outsiders, the sons of the grave, from whom the community has separated itself, must be regarded with caution and restraint. In fact, hatred is one's duty here. Humility and modesty are to be the hallmark of conduct within the

community. Chastity, already highly valued in official Judaism, leads
within the Qumran community on the one hand to the prohibition
of polygamy which was allowed in contemporary Judaism, and on
the other even to an order of male celibates. An important requirement made of members of the Qumran community is that they
should renounce all possessions. Material possessions are regarded as
spiritually dangerous. So the novice puts his possessions and his
earnings at the disposal of the community; false representations
about these are punishable. During the novice's incorporation into
the community, the community accepts these possessions of his as
their own, and these provide the means whereby a sparse, but
secure, minimum of food and clothing is guaranteed to the individual member of the community, as he now shares in the community of goods.

At the heart of the Qumran community is the observance of
cleanliness. It is true that purity of heart and conduct are also regarded as essential; they cannot be offset by ritual. But all the same,
ritual makes up a large part of the meaning of "cleanliness". Priests,
that is Aaronites of impeccable descent, take the first place in the
community: they play a decisive part in government; they bless
bread and wine at the common meal; the Teacher of Righteousness,
a leading figure of the community, is himself a priest. In Jerusalem
there are priests in office who are not of Aaronite descent, and
Levitical cleanliness is not observed there to the extent that is required at Qumran. So the Qumran community has cut itself off
from Temple worship at Jerusalem, though the intensity of this
separation varied from time to time and from group to group. In
the new world, when the present defects in Temple worship will be
rectified, the Qumran community will again join in those services
at the Jerusalem Temple which for the time being are suspended.

The essential feature of this cleanliness consists in repeated washings. The importance of these in the life of the member of the
Qumran community is borne out by the cisterns inside the order's
settlement. These bathings should not be referred to as "baptisms".
They are frequently repeated, and the first bathing is not regarded
as an initiation rite nor is it ever said to be specially important. The
novice is able to participate in these bathings as soon as he has completed his first year. The daily common meal however is open only
to full members of the community who have passed successfully
through the three-year novitiate and trial period. It has no sacra-

mental character and does not make use of any words of interpretation. Proceeding by lot plays an important part in the admission of the novice. After he has finally gained admission, the period of supervision is not over. Every year the learning and conduct of the members of the community are scrutinized, and there is discreet but intense spiritual examination by the members one of another as well as by the community leaders. And every year the position which a member occupies in the full chapter of the community is reviewed according to the religious perceptiveness and quality of life of the man in question. The life of the member of the community and his conduct in the chapter are subject to rules which are worked out casuistically in great detail. Infringement of them carries fixed penalties of varying severity. The community and chapter are directed by the priests and an "overseer". At first the community was much more democratically involved in this, but later special "judges" acquired a pre-eminent position.

The central significance which the cultic rituals held for the Qumran community is also apparent in their form of observance of the sabbath law. Ordinary Judaism had already become quite casuistically severe in this matter. One of the Qumran texts has twenty-eight detailed regulations on this particular commandment, and most of them keep to the standard of ordinary Judaism. But in characteristic points this normal standard is still exceeded in the Qumran community. For instance, on the sabbath it is forbidden to rescue cattle if they fall into a hole. This stricter observance of the sabbath at Qumran is matched by an independent Qumran calendar which deviates from that of official Judaism. The official calendar is aligned to the sun and the moon and numbers 354 days. The Qumran calendar on the other hand is completely solar and has 364 days, which means that, since 364 is divisible by seven, in the Qumran reckoning all the great festivals fall each year on the same day of the week. These days are Wednesdays, Fridays, and Saturdays. So the sabbath always stands apart and never overlaps another festival. There are indeed repeated reminders in the scrolls of the Qumran community not to move the regular feast days from their appointed places.

No one outside the Qumran community had access to these calendrical details or to the community rites which we mentioned above, the bathings and the common meal, as well as to much that we have yet to consider such as the eschatological hope and the form

6

of interpretation of the Old Testament in the light of this hope. For the Qumran scrolls regard their contents as secrets, as wisdom which, it is repeatedly urged, must be kept from outsiders and hidden from them. The practice of the Qumran community was, then, intensely esoteric. The members of the community gave their whole lives to the community and its teaching. In one scroll we read how one of their leaders, the Teacher of Righteousness, was publicly humiliated on the Day of Atonement, as reckoned by the Qumran calendar. Other members of the community too underwent derision and abuse. The community was a breeding ground for a distinct ethic of martyrdom. All this then is what a man opted for when he freely decided on entry into the Qumran community as the way in which he would live out his life.

How did a member of the Qumran community, committed to such a rigorous life, think of himself in relation to God? Many phrases in the Qumran writings express an extreme consciousness of sin: man as a furnace of sin, as a dwelling of darkness; man as dust, as a figure of clay, as flesh; he belongs to the wriggling heap of worms and becomes food for worms. Man is a sinner and an ignominious creature, and is lost in hopelessness. But God rescues him from this grave of hopelessness. He opens the sinner's mouth and heart; he lays bare his heart of dust. Thus man's salvation flows from God's mercy, from his acts of grace, his steadfast truth, his righteousness, his forgiveness, and his lovingkindness. "By thy goodness alone is man righteous and by thy many mercies", affirms the Qumran psalter, and this is not an isolated remark; the idea recurs quite often. The spirit which God has created for man and by which the member of the community can pray bestows true knowledge and leads him to righteous deeds, to righteous and blameless living, and to a firm stand in time of temptation. This means that God's saving work helps to establish the law; the man who has been thus forgiven no longer thinks of exchanging God's law for "smooth things", as do the hostile liars; that is, he no longer regards strict observance of the law with laxity or imprecision but takes it with complete seriousness. In short, the member of the Qumran community sees himself as a sinner through and through, and he knows that he is sustained solely by God's grace. But this grace proves to be effective precisely because it binds man to strict and fastidious observance of the law.

All that we have described so far—strict fulfilment of the law, severe consciousness of sin, and the experience of God's essential mercifulness—is set in a key which gives the whole Qumran outlook a distinct and unmistakable note. This key is the community's conviction that the end of the world with its mighty events is immediately at hand. And so strict observance of the law, sinfulness, and the gift of grace undergo a radical intensification. The Qumran scrolls, that is, are apocalyptic writings. The esoteric tendency which we have already noted in this community is here especially apparent, for outsiders know nothing of the details of this eschatological hope. The expectation is confined to the community. The intensity of the expectation does vary very considerably from text to text. Whenever the expectation is strongly in vogue, the conviction grows that the last days are breaking in here and now. The Qumran community does then see itself as the community of the last days. Its living members represent the last generation. The end, that is, is not simply *expected*. True, it has not yet fully arrived. The final end is still to come. But it will come to pass in this generation now living. This of course results in calculations being made, with all the consequences that such calculations inevitably bring with them: it is established that the end is delayed, hope weakens, the calculation is made again, the disappointment is overcome, and an attempt is made to hurry on the end.

The generation which lives under the shadow of the end is wicked. Special tempters appear: the "man of lies", two tempters in Jerusalem. The secrets of sin become the rage. After this there may be a flight brought on by the tribulations of the last days, the eschatological flight. The proximity of the end may bring the member of Qumran into particularly violent conflicts. Then the Holy War breaks out, the eschatological war against the adversaries of God who are led by Belial. The member of Qumran fights a spiritual battle, but he also wages it physically, in full armour and with all available weapons. In this last battle, the actions of men are assisted by the acts of God, for Michael supplies heavenly aid; the Messiah of Israel slays the adversary and the wicked spirits with the breath of his lips. The Last Judgement takes place. The elect take part in it. Then follows the punishment of the godless by fire. The world is destroyed by fire. Then the new creation comes to light. The Qumran community is there at the centre of it. With the destruction of the evil spirits the community is now finally cleansed; it is given the spiritual sprinkling of the last days and shares in the final redemption. Its members receive a share in the eternal council of the angels. The Jerusalem Temple of the last days is built with a ritually pure cult. No further destruction awaits it. In these last days the great eschatological saviours appear: the Teacher of Righteousness returns, and then a messianic prophet accompanied by two messiahs, the Messiah of Israel who has military functions and, superior to him, the priestly Messiah of Aaron. These messiahs are not thought of as pre-existent nor is there any mention of their suffering, their ascension, or their resurrection. In their presence the messianic meal is held, a meal of satiating abundance which had been anticipated in the daily meal of the Qumran community. There is no doctrine of the immortality of the soul in the Qumran community and this is probably true too of the resurrection of the body and indeed of the resurrection of the righteous only. Many individual details of the Qumran belief about the end have broadly Jewish characteristics about them. The conviction of living at the breaking-in of the last days and directly before their completion is a very specific feature of Qumran belief.

The conviction at Qumran that the end is near is so dominant that it provides the key to the way in which Old Testament texts are handled and interpreted by the Qumran community. When the member of Qumran reads his Old Testament, he sees in everything a reference to the last days and the eschatological community in which he lives. The prophets' words are fulfilled here and now. The Teacher of Righteousness knows more about the last days of the present than could the prophet Habakkuk in his day and age. So the Old Testament texts are applied by the Qumran community to the two messiahs that are expected, as well as to their prophet. Among the texts which have been discovered there is even a compilation of messianic texts extracted from the Old Testament. Scholars had long conjectured that a collection like this existed in Judaism and early Christianity, but now there is actual proof that this was so from this Qumran scroll. Above all, the member of Qumran sees reflected in the Old Testament the particular fortunes of his community as well as the events connected with the Teacher of Righteousness. The Old Testament is handled with amazing freedom at Qumran so as to squeeze from the text these references which are entirely foreign to the original. Changes are even made in the letters. Besides this the text is given new perspective and reference by the use of allegory. A distinctive style of interpretation is developed, the *pesher* method, in which a part of a verse is quoted and, with the repetition of particular words and ideas in the text, is given a free, allegorical interpretation. As a result, these expositions of the Old Testament, especially of the prophets, reach a height of fantasy and arbitrariness, compared with the original meaning—if indeed we want to make this the yardstick for assessing the interpretation given at Qumran. At the same time, this world of apocalyptic exegesis is not without a certain fascination and impressiveness even for the modern reader.

In conclusion, let me remind you that the picture I have given of the Qumran community has been intended to bring the time of Jesus into sharper focus. Can the New Testament be better understood with the help of the Qumran documents?

The answer to this is undoubtedly yes. In the New Testament there are expressions such as the "poor in spirit" in the first beatitude of the Sermon on the Mount or the "men with whom God is well pleased" in the message of the angels to the shepherds at Bethlehem, which had previously not been attested in the contemporary world of the New Testament. We now find these expressions in the Qumran scrolls and are better informed than before about their meaning. Added to this there are whole complexes of ideas where the New Testament has affinities with Qumran. In this context I must mention the distrust of possessions felt at Qumran, which is shared by the third Gospel and the Acts of the Apostles, but which otherwise is very un-Jewish; the tendency in some, though not all, New Testament writings to contrast life and death, light and darkness, and to talk in dualistic terms; the conviction of living at the breaking-in of the imminent end; and lastly the interpretation of the Old Testament in the light of this conviction. In all these ways the Qumran texts have affinities with the New Testament. The Qumran community represents a really serious attempt within Judaism to advance beyond the old position of Jewish belief, now found to be inadequate. The New Testament shares this aim with Qumran.

It is true that the way the two communities solved this attempt led to different results; and not just in matters of detail such as the two messiahs of Qumran and the one of the New Testament. Many more differences of detail could be mentioned. But the essential difference is this: the Qumran community did practise the Old Testament law in all its rigour, but they did not see that in this way man is inevitably lost again in self-glory. The God of Qumran helps the lost but then puts them on the path of the law where the pious man may be assured of salvation through meticulous obedience. The New Testament believes that a demand of this sort does not help the utterly lost. He can be helped only by the experience of love: this is how men are led to do what is right. In the Qumran documents there is nothing of the expansive outlook of Jesus, the unconditional friend of tax-gatherers and sinners, with whom you learn joyful and free obedience.

9 Temple and Synagogue

EDUARD LOHSE

When, as the Gospels tell us, Jesus stood with his disciples before the Temple in Jerusalem, they pointed out to him with great admiration how immense the building was: "Look, teacher, what wonderful stones and what wonderful buildings" (Mark 13.1 and parallels). The Temple was indeed an impressive spectacle which was begun in 20–19 B.C. and was ready for consecration after ten years' labour. But the great work went on for decades and was not completed until A.D. 64, shortly before the outbreak of the revolt against the Romans. If Herod hoped to receive thanks and recognition from the people for his action in providing a worthy edifice for the sacred place, he was to be singularly disappointed. The pious not only held it against their Idumean monarch that he ruled with an iron fist and went to ruthless lengths against his opponents; they, above all, could not forgive him for appearing to act like the prince of a Hellenistic state who tried to foster the good will of foreign cities with gifts, who patronized Greek sports and did not scruple to have votive offerings made even in pagan temples to bring honour to his name. Even so, no one could deny that he had done a great deal for the Jerusalem Temple, for not only did he have the Temple buildings reconstructed with particular regard to cultic requirements, but he also increased the Temple area to twice its former size, after he had secured the necessary extension by putting up retaining walls. A vast sum was spent on the enterprise, for no expense was spared. "Anyone who has not seen Herod's building has never seen anything beautiful" said a proverb. Some remains of this building activity can still be seen: the extensive Temple area is still there, just as it was laid out, and the Wailing Wall, as it is called, shows what Herod's architecture was like. This wall was not pulled down by the Romans after the fall of Jerusalem in A.D. 70, and was the place where the Jews were allowed to bewail the loss of the Temple.

All Jews, whether they lived in Palestine or were scattered throughout the Hellenistic world, shared the same longing to go to Jerusalem and pray in the place which God had chosen. Each of them made a contribution to it through the Temple tax—a double drachma per annum, roughly equivalent to the price of two sheep —so that the work and worship of the Temple might be carried on to the glory of God. Even the Qumran community, Jews who kept the law strictly and lived in the isolation of the desert by the shore of the Dead Sea, turned their eyes to Jerusalem. It was with pain that they had abandoned participation in the worship there, because in their view it was unclean. They looked for the coming of the Last Day when judgement would be carried out against the priests so that the Temple might be renewed and worship again conducted with priestly purity.

Anyone going up to Jerusalem could see the Temple from afar standing high on a rock, looking in the distance like a snow-covered hill in its brilliant splendour. If you had gone through the city gates and on up to the Temple area, you would first have come to the outer court, which was open even to Gentiles. On its Temple side this court was fenced off by a barrier on which warning notices were fixed. Written on them in Greek and Latin was: "No foreigner is allowed to go beyond the barrier and enclosure which surrounds the Temple. Anyone who is caught doing so will have himself to blame for his ensuing death." This warning was carefully respected even by the Roman occupation forces who had assumed power in A.D. 6, and any violation of the sacred area avoided. Behind this barrier was the inner court. Jewish women were allowed to enter its eastern part, but the western part was reserved for male Jews alone, for only they could take part in the cult. In front of the Temple stood the altar of burnt offerings; inside was the golden altar of incense, the seven-branched candlestick which was always kept alight, and the table of the shewbread on which twelve new loaves were laid each sabbath. The Holy of Holies, which was separated from the rest of the Temple by thick curtains, could be entered only by the high priest when he was to perform the act of expiation for Israel on the Day of Atonement. The Ark of the Covenant which had once stood on this spot in the

Temple of Solomon had been lost when Jerusalem was destroyed by the Babylonians in 587 B.C. When the Temple was rebuilt two generations later, this spot was left empty. So from that day forward the blood of the goat which was sacrificed by the high priest on the Great Day of Atonement for the sins of Israel was sprinkled over a stone on which the Ark had once stood, instead of over the Ark itself.

It was in the Temple that the priesthood carried out its duties. While the high priest and the chief priests were permanently resident in Jerusalem, most of the priests lived with their families outside the city in smaller country places. Their large number was divided up into twenty-four courses, as they were called, each of which was on duty for a week in turn. The priest and the Levite who followed him in the parable Jesus told of the Good Samaritan (Luke 10.30–7) were on their way home from Jerusalem to Jericho where they lived. They went home quickly and did not stop to help the man who had fallen among thieves and lay there beaten up on their route.

Any priest who was to offer a sacrifice had to meet the prescriptions of the law. He had to be free from any physical defect and not be unfit for the cultic act through any ritual uncleanness, contracted for instance by touching the corpse of a man or animal or through a bodily discharge. It was decided by lot among the priests which duties should be done by each. Before daybreak a herald would cry out: "Priests, begin your duties." There is a story that the Jewish king Agrippa who reigned over Palestine from A.D. 41–4 was once on a journey when he heard the herald's cry at a distance of three Persian miles, which is about ten English miles. Agrippa had gifts sent to the herald as a mark of appreciation. As soon as the priests heard the call they came hurrying to prepare for the punctual performance of the service. Every day an incense offering was burnt in the Temple and an unblemished one-year-old lamb sacrificed on the great altar of burnt offerings. In addition to this there were many private sacrifices from individual Jews who offered them as tokens of their thankfulness to God. Since pilgrims, who often came from long distances, were unable to bring with them an animal for sacrifice, facilities were provided in the forecourt of the Temple where they could buy an unblemished animal. This business gave rise to all sorts of trading, particularly since the Jews also had to change their money here into Tyrian coinage which was the traditional currency of the Temple.

On the great festivals—Passover in spring, Pentecost seven weeks later, then Tabernacles and the Day of Atonement in autumn—the city was packed with crowds of the faithful who had come to pray. The number of pilgrims on such days sometimes exceeded the population of Jerusalem, which was about 25,000. They were all able to find accommodation only because the inhabitants of the city had to provide hospitality for pilgrims from abroad free of charge, for Jerusalem is the property of all Israel. All Jews regard it as the holy city, the centre of Israel, and indeed of the whole earth. Anyone who prays here receives a special blessing for, as it says somewhere, it is as though he were praying before the throne of glory, because here are the gate of heaven and the door open to prayer.

Even in the spring of A.D. 70, despite the revolt against the Romans, many Jews had come to Jerusalem to keep the Passover there. Along with the inhabitants of the city they were surprised and shut in by the advancing Roman troops, so that very soon the distress of the crowds was almost unendurable. But right until the end the sacrificial worship in the Temple was discharged with punctilious fidelity and the hope maintained that the holy place would not fall into the hands of the Gentiles. The last bands of rebels retreated inside the Temple area and put up a bitter resistance until the building went up in flames. And so Judaism lost its visible centre in the world. But even so it managed to survive this frightful catastrophe and continue its existence right until the present day. And this was possible because the religious life of the Jews was not tied to the Temple cultus only but derived strength and support from other sources. There was still the law of God, and this was read and expounded in the synagogues where the Jewish communities met together both in Palestine and in the *diaspora*.

The beginnings of the synagogue are lost in obscurity. The first definite evidence for Jewish synagogues comes from the third century B.C. But it may be taken for certain that there had been synagogues in earlier times. Their origin is to be sought in the *diaspora* where the Jews lived scattered among peoples of different beliefs. In these foreign parts, far from their homeland, they had to make for themselves a place where they could meet for the worship of God. It is quite likely that the Jews who had been carried off to Babylon after the fall of Jerusalem in 587 b.c. and had to live there in exile erected places where they could hear the word and commandment of God, but there is no definite evidence of this. Synagogues were then rapidly established in all parts of the diaspora and even in Palestine, so that by Jesus' day there was a synagogue in every place where Jews were living. In the bigger cities such as Jerusalem, Rome, Alexandria, or Antioch, there were several synagogues where congregations held their services, the law was studied, and the children given instruction. The connection between the law and the synagogue was accepted as so natural by the Jews of New Testament times that it was thought that there had always been synagogues since the days of Moses. Thus in the Acts of the Apostles we read at one point: "From early generations Moses has had in every city those who preach him, for he is read every sabbath in the synagogues" (Acts 15.21).

Throughout the Roman empire the synagogue enjoyed official recognition and civil protection. So even outside Palestine the Jews were able to avail themselves quite freely of the right to free assembly; their congregations could own property, practise alms-giving, administer their own finances, establish their own grave-yards, and even conduct their own justice. The administration of the external affairs of a synagogue was in the hands of a committee which as a rule consisted of three members. The leadership of the synagogue congregation was vested in the president of the synagogue who first and foremost was responsible for the regular ordering of the services. He was assisted by the synagogue attendant who had to see to the ordinary round of duties and, should the occasion arise, carry out synagogue punishments such as the administration of scourging to anyone who had violated the law. Otherwise, there were no permanent officials, for all liturgical functions were carried out by members of the congregation.

The house in which the congregation met was usually designed as a long, rectangular building, orientated towards Jerusalem. At its entrance stood jars of water, so that everyone going into the synagogue could carry out the ritual cleansing. The prayer hall was kept plain and simple; the scrolls stood in a niche and were brought out at worship. Before the service could begin there had to be at least ten men present; a smaller number was not enough to constitute a congregation for worship.

The shape of the service has remained the same in its funda-
mentals from the time of Jesus until now. It divides into two parts.
The first is decidedly liturgical in character and begins with Israel's
confession of the One God. This is made up of three extracts from
Numbers and Deuteronomy and is recited daily by every faithful
Jew. It is introduced by the summons: "Hear, O Israel; the Lord
our God is one Lord" (Deut. 6.4), and then recalls the commandments and acts of God which his people profess. Then follow the
prayers known as the Eighteen Benedictions which comprise
eighteen blessings and intercessions; part of the text of this had
already been fixed by New Testament times. The first three
phrases and the last three are exhortations to praise God. "Blessed
art thou, O Lord, God of Abraham, God of Isaac and God of
Jacob; the most high God, creator of heaven and earth, our shield
and the shield of our fathers." "Thou art our champion, the
strong one, the eternal who raisest the dead, carest for the living
and quickenest the dead." "Holy art thou and fearful thy name;
there is no God but thee. Blessed art thou, O Lord, the holy God."
A prayer-leader spoke these sentences and the congregation replied Amen, which means: "Surely", thereby making their own
what was said in the prayer. The blessings at the beginning and
the end of the prayer provide the framework for the petitions
which refer not only to daily needs but also to the messianic era,
praying that God, in his mercy, may bring it in. Between the last
two blessings there is the benediction: "The Lord bless you and
keep you . . ." (Num. 6.24–6). If a priest was present at the synagogue service, he had to give this benediction. But when there
was no priest there the benediction was said by a member of the
congregation in the form of a prayer addressed to God. Again the
congregation answered Amen. Then the first part of the service
ended with the eighteenth blessing: "Give thy peace to thy people
Israel and bless us all. Blessed art thou, O Lord, who makest
peace. Amen."

The second part of the service is didactic. It contains readings
from the law (that is the Pentateuch) and from the prophets, and
includes a sermon if there is anyone in the assembled congregation
able to give an exposition of the word which has been read.
Every male Jew was entitled to take an active part in the conduct
of the service. But to preserve order the synagogue president

through the attendant called on each in turn to step forward and lead the prayers, read the scroll of scripture, or preach.

Like any other Jew, Jesus and his disciples were free to take the floor in the synagogue and speak to the congregation. In St Luke's Gospel we have a good picture of how the service proceeded in Jesus' home town of Nazareth. Jesus went into the synagogue on the sabbath and stood up to read. The scroll of the prophet Isaiah was handed to him by the attendant, and from it Jesus read the first two verses of chapter 61:

> The Spirit of the Lord is upon me, because he has anointed me to preach good news to the poor. He has sent me to proclaim release to the captives and recovering of sight to the blind, to set at liberty those who are oppressed, to proclaim the acceptable year of the Lord.

To the great amazement of his hearers, the sermon which Jesus then added consisted of only one sentence: "Today this scripture has been fulfilled in your hearing" (Luke 4.16–21).

The rights which the synagogue enjoyed in the Roman empire remained intact even after the Jewish war. So the congregations were able to continue meeting for the praise of God and the study of the scriptures and to live as Jews in the midst of a world of many creeds and beliefs. The memory of the destroyed Temple was kept alive in the synagogue service. The people assembled in the morning and the afternoon at the times when the daily sacrifice had previously been offered in the Temple, a seven-branched candlestick became a part of the furnishing of the synagogue, and the hope was kept alive that one day Israel would be able to return to its lost centre. The prayers continually ask God that it may please him "to dwell in Zion so that thy servants may serve thee in Jerusalem" (the sixteenth of the Eighteen Benedictions). And year after year the Passover is concluded with the wish: "Next year in Jerusalem."

The synagogues which sprang up everywhere around the Mediterranean in both large and small places made a marked impression on the people living near them. In many places this led to hostility towards the Jews, but in the days of Jesus there is no doubt that the synagogue attracted far more than it repelled. Many were impressed by the simple worship in which there were no images of God and no sacrifices. Venerable writings were read and their content considered by the group. So to many non-Jews the gathering in the synagogue 'virtually looked like a circle of people trained in philosophy who were meeting to study the writings after the fashion of the wise men of old. Many wanted to know something more about the beliefs of the Jews and came to the synagogue to learn more of their detail. But full admission to Judaism was impeded by the requirement that a man must be circumcized and adopt the whole law including its ritual demands. The Jews for their part, however, tried to meet the hesitations of the Gentiles halfway by requiring them to keep only the most important and fundamental commandments, such as the observance of the sabbath, the food regulations, and the moral precepts, along with the confession of the One God. Anyone who undertook these requirements was regarded as a God-fearer. Although in law he remained one of his own people and was not a Jew, he belonged to the synagogue in a loose association. So when the first Christian missionaries, who were mostly of Jewish origin, proclaimed in the synagogues that Jesus of Nazareth was the Anointed of God and the ground of salvation for all the world, they often received a much more ready hearing among these God-fearers than in the congregation proper of the synagogue. The fact that it was not necessary to be circumcized and adopt the law, but that Jews and Gentiles alike were invited to accept Jesus as Lord, made it all the more easy for them to join the nascent Christian congregations.

Jewish worship, whether in the Temple or in the synagogue, is a sacred act and so is separated from anything profane by rigorous limits. A sacrificial animal had to be without blemish and not be put to ordinary use. Ritual cleanliness is a strict prerequisite for performing cultic actions, and sacred times are sharply separated from the profane. The Christian Church, whose origins are closely connected with the synagogue, does not acknowledge this discrimination in cult and ritual. It is open to Jew and Gentile alike, because there can no longer be any separation between men who share in acknowledging the one God and Lord. Every man who belongs to Christ and is marked as his possession by baptism is holy. The whole Church, which belongs to God alone and so must live a holy life—that is, a life in accordance with God's commandments—is a priestly people. Thus Paul says to the Church: "God's temple is holy, and that temple you are" (1 Cor. 3.17). Among the people of God, who are called together from all nations, all the barriers created by men are torn and and a temple erected not made with hands. This large band is exhorted by the apostle in the Epistle to the Romans to present their bodies—and that means themselves, with all that they are and have—as a sacrifice which may be living, holy, and acceptable to God (Rom. 12.1). In this way the whole of life is incorporated into the worship of God which is carried on in the midst of the daily life of the world, for God's Church knows itself to be bound to obedience and proves "what is the will of God, what is good and acceptable and perfect" (Rom. 12.2).

10 Jesus and his Disciples

JOSEF BLINZLER

When Jesus of Nazareth began to proclaim the kingdom of God in the towns and villages of Galilee, he presented each person in the crowd, to whom his call came, with a decision. One section, chiefly the group made up of the religious and political leaders, reacted with scepticism, with unconcealed distrust, then with flat rejection, and finally with deadly hostility. Others immediately received the message of the messianic kingdom eagerly and attentively, but then lost all interest when it became clear that Jesus' idea of the kingdom of God had nothing in common with their own. But right from the start there were people who were deeply moved by his words and deeds, who willingly listened to him and opened their hearts to his message, flocked to him with joy and enthusiasm and accompanied him wherever he went. Within this large circle of followers and adherents there was a further definable group formed by the disciples.

The word "disciple" is traditionally used to translate the Greek word used in the Gospels, *mathētēs*, which means apprentice or pupil. If we want to understand aright the particular nature of discipleship in the New Testament, we must first look at the parallels of language and content among the Greeks and the Jews.

The Greeks as a rule used the word *mathētēs* (which first occurs in Herodotus iv. 77) of someone who under the expert tuition of a teacher or master acquired a certain technical or intellectual knowledge or facility, like the trade-apprentice or the pupil of an orator or philosopher. In addition to this the word was also sometimes used in cases where there was no personal relationship between pupil and teacher, but only an ideal, timeless affinity, so that, for instance, Socrates came to be called the *mathētēs* of Homer (so

Dio Chrysostom). As with the word *didaskalos*, or teacher, the prime emphasis in the word *mathētēs*, pupil, is not on the intellectual link but on the external tie, rather after the nature of a business relationship or apprenticeship. This explains why Socrates refused to let himself be called a teacher or his companions *mathētai*, as was the custom of the sophists who accepted payment for their instruction. Socrates saw his relationship with his pupils as a partnership between one intellect that gives and another that receives. Plato and Xenophon still avoid calling the circle around Socrates his pupils and make use of various circumlocutions. Later writers prefer to say "his intimate companions" (*gnōrimoi*), which clearly expresses the idea of partnership with the teacher rather than dependence on him. There is the same emphasis of meaning in the German *Jünger* (disciple, literally the younger one) as compared with the word *Schüler* (pupil). The relationship between master and disciple took on a particularly intimate, almost religious, character with the Pythagoreans, the Epicureans, and the followers of Apollonius of Tyana.

The Hebrew equivalent of *mathētēs* is the word *talmid*. Surprisingly, it plays virtually no part in the Old Testament and the same is true of *mathētēs* in its Greek translation, the Septuagint. "Unlike the classical Greek and Hellenistic world... the Old Testament does not know a master–disciple relationship. Neither the writings of the prophets nor those of the scribes of the Old Testament contain any such idea" (K.-H. Rengstorf). In a milieu of revelation there is no place for such a relationship to develop. For the Old Testament prophets the master and teacher is God himself. In rabbinic thinking, on the other hand, there are many references to the *talmid*. But although the verb *lamad*, "to learn", is used of learning a trade, *talmid* never means a trade apprentice but always someone who is engaged in studying the scriptures and religious traditions. Private study of the Torah did not make one a *talmid*: one had first to be attached to a teacher, or *rab*. The pupils, gathered round the rabbi in the classroom (all of them like him in a sitting position), listened to the words of the teacher, put questions to him, and memorized what they heard by continual repetition. Eliezer ben Hyrcanus is celebrated in tradition for having preserved the words of his teacher as faithfully "as a lime-washed cistern, which does not let one drop of water escape". But they were expected to learn how to live according to the Torah

7

not only from the teacher's words but also from his life. With this
in view, they made themselves his servants. They were exempt
only from particularly menial jobs such as unfastening his sandal
straps. When out and about, as befitted subordinates, they would
walk behind their teacher at an appropriate distance, while he
either went on foot or rode on a donkey. Thus they "followed"
him quite literally. A circle of pupils acquired from their teacher
a distinct character, both outwardly and inwardly, so that it is
possible to talk of individual "schools". The best known were the
schools of Hillel and Shammai and later that of Akiba. As a member of a school, each pupil was a representative of his rabbi's
tradition. The late Jewish *talmid*-institute appears to have developed under Greek influence, for schools, in the sense of communities of disciples in which the principle of tradition was hon-
oured, were characteristic of the Hellenistic world.

At first sight the way Jesus acted seems very similar to the be-
haviour of a rabbi, and his relationship with his disciples very
like that between the rabbis and their pupils. Like a rabbi Jesus
claims that he is proclaiming the will of God; he appears in the
synagogues as a teacher; he participates in discussions about the
meaning of scripture and about certain doctrines; he knows and
uses the techniques of rabbinic argument; he is occasionally invited by Pharisees to dine with them or is approached about a
decision in a lawsuit; he is given the respectful address of "rabbi";
and it is certainly no accident that the Talmud uses of Jesus'
disciples the word *talmidim* which is otherwise used only of the
pupils of the rabbis.

But we must also notice the differences. Jesus does not assemble
a regular group of pupils in the classroom. He also teaches not just
in the synagogue but usually anywhere in the open, in public
places, on the seashore, in the fields, on the hillside, or while
walking. He cannot say that he is the pupil of a famous rabbi,
as the rabbis did with pride. On the contrary, he was regarded as
a man without a formal education (Mark 6.2f; John 7.15). His way
of teaching was fundamentally different from the rabbinic method.
He never cited any of the earlier authorities for support, as was
rabbinic custom. While the scribe regarded the exposition of the
Torah as his particular and principal task, Jesus claimed for himself the authority to discern the will of God independently of the
scriptures and the right to decide whether in a particular case the

Torah really was the pure expression of the will of God or not. This explains why the disciples never appear as partners in discussion with Jesus, putting questions and raising objections, as was the practice in the teaching methods of the rabbis. A rabbi never talked as Jesus did in the antitheses of the Sermon on the Mount or in his answer about divorce (Mark 10.2–9). Neither did any of the prophets, who had always only to transmit the word of God. The authority which Jesus displayed in his teaching was quickly seen to be the fundamental factor which marked him off from the way the rabbi taught (Mark 1.22).

As with the rabbis, Jesus' relationship with his disciples was also not just an association of teacher and learner. It was in addition a community of personal fellowship. The rabbis regarded this community life from the outset as only temporary; it came to an end when the pupil had finished his apprenticeship and had become an independent rabbi. But Jesus' disciples were not released from their relationship as followers and they did not move on to the status of independent teacher or master. In a few sayings of Jesus in the synoptic tradition there are still distinct echoes of this idea. "But you are not to be called rabbi, for you have one teacher and you are all brethren" (Matt. 23.8). "A disciple is not above his teacher, nor a servant above his master; it is enough for this disciple to be like his teacher, and the servant like his master" (Matt. 10.24f). "Like his teacher"—this certainly does not mean that the disciple eventually becomes of similar standing to his teacher; but that he must be prepared to share the lot of his teacher —humiliation, contempt, persecution, and death.

More significant still is the difference in the way the teacher–disciple relationship originated. The rabbinic pupils selected as their teacher anyone in their neighbourhood from the vast numbers of scribes of their day whom they esteemed and admired as an authority in the knowledge of the Torah. "Choose a teacher and take a companion [for study together]" was what was impressed on the young Israelite from about 100 B.C. (Aboth 1.6). In the second century A.D. Rabban Gamaliel was still repeating the exhortation in a slightly altered form: "Choose a teacher and you rise above doubt", by which he meant, "Only under the direction of a teacher can you reach any certainty of knowledge and perception." In contrast, you became a disciple of Jesus not by choosing him as your teacher but by his calling you. The traditions are unanimous about this. This is Mark's account of the call of the first disciples:

> And passing along by the Sea of Galilee, he saw Simon and Andrew the brother of Simon casting a net in the sea; for they were fishermen. And Jesus said to them, "Follow me and I will make you become fishers of men." And immediately they left their nets and followed him (1.16f).

In the same way he immediately went on to call James and John, and on other occasions Levi/Matthew (Mark 2. 13f), Philip (John 1.43), and others (Luke 9.59; Mark 10.21). So the Fourth Gospel has Jesus say: "You did not choose me, but I chose you" (John 15.16). The stories of these callings are certainly in accord with the conclusion that the decisive initiative in becoming a disciple came from Jesus, although these narratives are not historical accounts, as is shown by the schematic form in which they are told. The intention behind them is rather to make clear what discipleship basically means: that it is being caught by Christ. In fact, becoming a disciple was not a spontaneous decision made on the spur of the moment. There was a prehistory to each of the stories of the calls. And this can still be seen in the case of Simon and Andrew. According to John's Gospel, Jesus won over five men, among them these two brothers, while he was still with John the Baptist in the region of the Jordan 1.35–42).

A further indication that one became a disciple by being called is afforded by those instances where people actually offered to follow Jesus. A man who had been healed of demon-possession asked him if he could stay with him, but he was turned away: "Go home to your friends, and tell them how much the Lord has done for you, and how he has had mercy on you" (Mark 5.18f). Two others, who assured him "I will follow you wherever you go", were soberly reminded of the greatness of the sacrifice which discipleship involved (Luke 9.57,61). Following Jesus, that is, involved a radical renunciation of almost everything which is commonly thought of as making life worth living. It meant giving up one's previous occupation. The stories of the calls insist on this emphatically: "And immediately they left their nets" (Mark 1. 18). "And they left their father Zebedee in the boat with the hired servants" (1.20). "And [Levi/Matthew] rose [from the tax-office] and followed him" (2.14). There is a hint of the difficulty which such a decision meant in a remark of Peter's later on: "Lo, we

have left everything and followed you" (Mark 10.28). "Everything", he says with justice. For following Jesus meant for him
and his companions leaving their families. Jesus demands that the
disciple subordinate his ties with his parents, wife, and children
to the tie with himself. "If any one comes to me and does not hate
his own father and mother and wife and children and brothers
and sisters, yes, and even his own life, he cannot be my disciple"
(Luke 14.25f). A quite staggering demand! But "hate" is a
Semitism and means no more than "deliberately set aside". Jesus
did not abrogate the fourth commandment but expressly affirmed
it (Mark 10.19; 7.10–12). The meaning of the saying is more
clearly expressed in Matthew's version: "He who loves father or
mother more than me is not worthy of me; and he who loves son
or daughter more than me is not worthy of me" (10.37). No matter
how important filial obligations to parents are, following Jesus
comes first. One man to whom the call of Jesus came asked for a
brief postponement: "Let me first go and bury my father." But
Jesus told him: "Leave the dead to bury their own dead; but as
for you, go and proclaim the kingdom of God" (Luke 9.59f).
Someone else exclaimed: "I will follow you, Lord; but let me first
say farewell to those at my home", to which Jesus replied: "No
one who puts his hand to the plow and looks back is fit for the
kingdom of God" (Luke 9.61f). The farmer as he ploughs should
not look back if he wants his furrows to be straight. In the same
way, a man is fit for the disciple's task of proclaiming the kingdom
of God only if he is wholeheartedly devoted to it and does not
look back at what he has left behind.

Following Jesus meant renouncing marriage. Jesus speaks of
this in a strange saying recorded in Matthew (19.11f). It occurs in
the context of a remark about those who are not married, and
refers to others "who have made themselves eunuchs for the sake
of the kingdom of heaven". In contrast with the Essenes, for instance, who rejected marriage for Gnostic and dualistic reasons,
this saying talks of celibacy "for the sake of the kingdom of
heaven". This can only mean: "in order to be free to proclaim
the kingdom of heaven".

Following Jesus also meant renouncing personal possessions. A
rich young man is invited to follow him with the words: "You
lack one thing; go, sell what you have, and give to the poor, and
you will have treasure in heaven; and come, follow me" (Mark

10.21). The promise of being rewarded a hundredfold is made to those who have left their families as well as their houses and lands for his sake (Mark 10.28–30). "Whoever of you does not renounce all that he has cannot be my disciple", we read in Luke 14.33. The disciples are sent out on their mission without money in their belts (Mark 6.8 with variations in Matthew and Luke). John mentions twice that Jesus and his disciples had a common purse which was kept by Judas (John 12.6; 13.29). The members of the Qumran sect, after a two-year novitiate, also had to give away their possessions to the community, the "congregation of the poor". But whatever the reason for this practice, the renunciation of possessions by Jesus' disciples was different, because for them the real purpose of poverty was to make them as free as possible for service of the kingdom of God.

Following Jesus meant, finally, being prepared to share the lot of the master, accepting homelessness, suffering, hatred, persecution, and even death. "Foxes have holes, and birds of the air have nests; but the Son of man has nowhere to lay his head" (Luke 9.58; Matt. 8.19). "A disciple is not above his teacher, nor a servant above his master; it is enough for the disciple to be like his teacher, and the servant like his master. If they have called the master of the house Beelzebul, how much more will they malign those of his household" (Matt. 10.24f). "Beware of men; for they will deliver you up to councils, and flog you in their synagogues, and you will be dragged before governors and kings for my sake.... And you will be hated by all for my name's sake. But he who endures to the end will be saved" (Matt. 10.17f, 22). "You will be delivered up even by parents and brothers and kinsmen and friends, and some of you they will put to death" (Luke 21.16; cf. also Matt. 23.34–9).

So in the end the disciple is asked to be ready for nothing less than martyrdom. "If any man would come after me, let him deny himself and take up his cross and follow me" (Mark 8.34; cf. Matt. 16.24; Luke 9.23; cf. Matt. 10.38; Luke 14.27). To deny oneself means no longer following the emotions, the wishes, the dreams of one's own ego, but being led solely by the will of God, as heard and acknowledged in the call of Jesus. "For whoever would save his life will lose it; and whoever loses his life for my sake and the gospel's will save it" (Mark 8.35). If anyone suffers death out of faithfulness to his Lord, he saves his real life and finds eternal salvation; but it is forfeited by the man who is able to save his miserable earthly life by denying his master. "Salt is good; but if salt has lost its taste, how shall its saltness be restored? It is fit neither for the land nor for the dunghill; men throw it away" (Luke 14.34–5). A disciple in whom the spirit of uncompromising loyalty to Christ and readiness to die for him has evaporated is worthless, like salt that has become tasteless. "Men throw it away"—a warning hint of the fate that awaits those who break faith. But the man who holds out to the end within the fellowship is promised by Jesus a special share in his kingdom (Luke 22.29f; Matt. 19.28; cf. Luke 10.20; John 8.31f).

An undertaking which demands such an unprecedented degree of sacrifice can only be attempted after the most thorough self-examination. This is the meaning of the double parable of the Tower Builder and the King going to War (Luke 14.28–32). Jesus will have no one around him who cannot be relied on; he does not want enthusiasts who are all fire and flame, who leave everything and go along with him but then tire of this sacrificial service and miserably fail. John 6.60–71 shows that this was a real danger, for there we are told that at the time of the "Galilean crisis" many disciples left him and no longer went along with him. This was why, in that double parable, he so strongly advised those who did not feel equal to the responsibilities of discipleship not to think of attempting to follow him.

But can it not be objected that everyone to whom Jesus' call came had a duty to follow him? No, following Jesus in the sense that we have outlined was not demanded of everyone. In the double parable, Jesus has in mind only that sort of discipleship which his permanent companions and fellow workers undertook. The particular demands he laid on them to renounce everything were connected with the particular task for which he had chosen them, the task of service in the kingdom of God.

He had already spoken of this task in the metaphor with which he called Simon and Andrew away from their nets: "I will make you become fishers of men". He intends to school them so that they are capable of winning men for the coming kingdom of God. That is why Mark's account of the call of the twelve distinguishes between a present and future appointment: "He appointed twelve, to be with him, and to be sent out to preach and have authority to cast out demons" (Mark 3.14–15). As his permanent companions they were the privileged witnesses of his words and miracles; they alone were initiated into the secret of the kingdom of God (Mark 4.10f; cf. 7.17–23; 10.10–12), into the messianic secret (8.30), and the secret of his suffering (8.31; 9.30f; 10.32f). Admittedly, tradition does not hide the fact that even so they continually failed to understand him aright and in the end all forsook him when he was arrested in Gethsemane. Not until after Easter was the circle of disciples to be reconstituted—by the risen Christ himself (Luke 24.26f,44–9; Acts 1.8; Matt. 28.16–20; John 20.24–9; cf. 2.22; 12.16), who indicated the new, more intimate relationship he has with his disciples by calling them his "brethren" (Matt. 28.10; John 20.17).

So the first task of the disciples after they had been called was for them to be trained for their future vocation. Then, after some time Jesus sent them out preaching the kingdom of God to all Israel and endowed them with a share in his own authority—the authority to drive out demons and heal the sick (Mark 6.6–13 and parallels), and even with his own divine authority: "He who hears you hears me, and he who rejects you rejects me, and he who rejects me rejects him who sent me" (Luke 10.16). Lastly, they were sent out by the risen Christ to proclaim the gospel throughout all the world (Matt. 28.16f; Luke 24.48f; Acts 1.8).

We must not think, then, of the hard demands which Jesus made on his disciples in terms of the proclamation of a new ascetic ideal, of a sort of super-ethic. Nor should they be thought of as an esoteric way to salvation or even as the one and only way. They are merely conditions of the work, qualifications for the office of ambassador of the gospel. Those among Jesus' adherents who were not disciples were not required to give away all their possessions. Zacchaeus, the chief tax-collector, kept the greater part of his wealth even after his conversion (Luke 19.1–10), and similarly the Galilean women who supported Jesus clearly continued to have private means at their disposal (Luke 8.1–3). When the early Church tried at first to organize some sort of community of goods (Acts 2.44f; 4.34f), it was not because they felt that they had to do this in obedience to a command of their Lord, for handing over all you had for the needs of the Church was voluntary (5.4) and not universal (4.36f). Nor did Jesus want everyone to renounce his family and marriage. On the contrary he explained: "Not all men can receive this precept, but only those to whom it is given"

(Matt. 19.11). It is true that no clear distinction is drawn in the Gospels between the demands made of out-and-out followers and the requirements laid on all believers, such as the new commands of the Sermon on the Mount (Matt. 5.21–48), particularly the command to love your neighbour, as well as unflinching witness to Christ (Mark 8.38). But this can be explained by the fact that the words of Jesus were originally handed down out of their historical context and that the Gospels were put together at a time when following Jesus in the sense of living in direct contact with him was no longer possible, for this presupposed the bodily presence of Jesus. In consequence, his sayings about discipleship came to be applied to Christians in general and the word "disciple" gradually acquired the meaning of a "Christian" (e.g. Acts 6.1,2,7; 9.1,10).

But in what way are the terms "disciple", "apostle", and "the twelve" related to one another? The facts of the matter are extremely complicated. Sometimes when the Gospels talk of disciples they mean just the twelve whom Jesus chose from the throng of his adherents at some point in his ministry which we are no longer able to determine precisely (cf. Mark 14.12 with 14.17). But in general they refer to the larger circle of people whom Jesus made his constant companions and sent on the mission to Israel after a period of preparation. It is true that Mark tells of only *one* mission of the twelve (6.6–13), but Luke follows his account of the mission of the twelve (9.1–6) with a parallel account a little further on of a mission of seventy or seventy-two disciples (10.1–16). This suggests that there was only one mission of the disciples and that it comprised a far larger circle, the size of which cannot be determined since the number seventy or seventy-two in the tradition is merely intended as a round figure. Even so, the theory which is widely canvassed nowadays, that the group of twelve was not appointed by Jesus, cannot be right. The post-resurrection community would surely not have included the traitor Judas in this group, and moreover the oldest tradition going back to the primitive Church knows of an appearance of the risen Christ to the twelve (1 Cor. 15.5; cf. also the supplementary election of Matthias, Acts 1.15–26). The number twelve is no doubt a symbolic reference to the twelve tribes of Israel. For Jesus the circle of the twelve represents and constitutes the new people of God living in the last days. .

We are accustomed nowadays to speak of the twelve apostles. This way of speaking goes back to Luke (6.13; 22.14), but it does not accord with the usage of the older Gospels, for Mark and Matthew regularly talk of "the twelve" or "the twelve disciples" and use the title "apostle" only in the context of the disciples' being sent out on the mission (Mark 6.30; Matt. 10.2). Apostle in fact means just that: "one who is sent", "ambassador". In many cases we know nothing more of the individual members of the group of twelve than their names, and even then the "lists of apostles" sometimes differ. The figure of Simon Peter is the most sharply drawn. He is the spokesman of the other disciples, to whom Jesus gave the nickname "rock" (Cephas, Peter), not because of his character which was, in fact, vacillating, passionate, and impulsive, but because of the position to which he was destined and appointed—of being the foundation of the Church (Matt. 16.18f). The two sons of Zebedee, James and John, also emerge with some clarity. They acquired the nickname of the "sons of thunder", doubtless because of their violent, impetuous nature. Together with Peter they make up the even smaller circle of three intimate apostles who, for example, were alone allowed to witness the raising of Jairus' daughter, the transfiguration, and the agony in Gethsemane. Levi/Matthew was originally a tax-collector and, because of this, shunned in society and religion. Simon Zealotes came, as his second name indicates, from the radical nationalist party of Zealots. The fact that men of such divergent backgrounds —Zealot and tax-collector, partisan and collaborator—found their way to Jesus shows what a compelling personality Jesus must have had. Probably none of the disciples came from the upper classes. They were mostly Galilean fishermen, and very likely craftsmen and farmers too. The only non-Galilean was, it would seem, Judas Iscariot, and this fact makes it a little easier to understand his particular position, although he has been swallowed up in obscurity and not even poetic fancy has been able to shed any light on this sinister figure, nor is it ever likely to.

Jesus' sayings about discipleship were first spoken at a particular time, in a particular situation, to particular people. Even so, thousands of people since then have accepted them as the personal call of God to themselves. In A.D. 270 a rich Copt aged 20 heard at service the words: "If you would be perfect, go, sell what you possess and give to the poor ... and come, follow me" (Matt.

19.21). They went straight to his heart, so that he at once acted on them quite literally, giving away all his possessions and retiring into the solitude of the desert for prayer and work. We know and honour him today as Antony the Great, the patriarch of monasticism. On the 24 February 1209 the son of an Umbrian merchant, Francis of Assisi, heard read at mass in the church of St Mary of the Angels the words in which Jesus told his disciples not to take any worldly goods on their mission. Francis accepted what he heard as a command from God directed specifically at him. He discarded shoes, staff, bag, and money and began to preach the gospel as a poor man amongst the poor. The biblical idea of the following or Imitation of Christ, which was also held by the primitive Church, inspired an unknown writer of the fifteenth century to produce the little book of that name, which became, and still remains, one of the most widely read and beloved of devotional writings. So too, Jesus' directions to his disciples will move men in the future also and induce them to follow Christ in ways appropriate to their times. For no matter how far the process of dechristianization goes in the world, there will always be men and women who like the disciples of John's Gospel, when asked by Jesus "Will you also go away?" will answer: "Lord, to whom shall we go? You have the words of eternal life" (John 6.68).

11 The Miracles of Jesus against their Contemporary Background

ANTON VÖGTLE

Readers of an article on miracles may well expect me first of all to try to give an unimpeachable definition of miracle based on current ideas of the laws of nature. Following on from this, they may think that I should give my view particularly on the problem whether it is possible to establish the existence of a miracle at all. But if I am not very much mistaken, our topic dispenses us from dealing with these preliminary questions. Let me give two reasons why this is so.

In the first place, the world of the New Testament did not share the modern concept of the laws of nature, whether in the sense of an absolute determinism or in the more relative sense of a statistical regularity. There was no tendency in the way the world was then conceived to distinguish as sharply as we do between an event explicable in natural terms and an effect which is inexplicable in terms of the forces and laws of nature. This means that the thinking of the ancient world, and even more biblical belief about God, did not call in question whether an extraordinary event was possible or actually happened just because it broke or went beyond the laws of nature as then known or presumed. So in the Old Testament even a completely natural and everyday event, like the wind blowing in a favourable direction or a battle ending in victory before sunset, could be regarded in a particular situation as a "miracle", as a remarkable demonstration of the power and love of God, because it changed the way in which it was thought or feared that things would turn out. The second reason is that I am to talk not about the concept of miracle in general but about actual miracles which in the Gospel tradition are linked with the person of Jesus, about narratives of particular events which provoked astonishment or sounded quite unbelievable—as we may put it with reference to the etymology of the word "miracle", without thereby postulating a concept of miracle based on a scientific understanding of reality.

The New Testament does connect with the figure of Jesus a great variety of wonderful events which for the most part we can understand and describe, in the light of our experience and use of language, only as miracles such as we have not heard of before, going beyond all that we at any rate can think or conceive of. There are, first of all, the miracles ascribed to the earthly life of Jesus as having been experienced by him or as having happened to him—such as the virgin birth of Jesus in the infancy narratives (themselves full of individual miracles too), the voice from heaven at the baptism of Jesus by the Jordan, the transfiguration, the resurrection, the resurrection appearances, and the ascension. Then there are all the wonderful events which are represented as still to come, beginning with the coming of the Son of man with or on the clouds of heaven to judge the world. All miraculous events of this sort fall beyond the scope of this article, even though the way they are presented also needs to be seen against the background of their day. In particular they need to be seen against the background of contemporary hopes of redemption, if we are to discover what these images really mean, what actually did happen and is still to happen, and to what extent the events they depict are to be taken literally, by which we mean how far they are identical with the realities they refer to.

We are concerned here only with those miracles which the Gospels show Jesus himself as performing during his public ministry: driving out demons, healing the sick, and the so-called nature miracles. It has long been recognized that we can only really understand and evaluate these miracle stories too if we are prepared to take the trouble to look at them against their contemporary background. For they are by no means the only ones of their day. The Jewish and Hellenistic worlds also had their miracle workers and miracle stories. It must be said that apart from practices connected with exorcism, that is driving out demons which were thought to be the cause of physical and mental illnesses, we hear next to nothing of miracle workers and specific miracle stories from Jewish Palestine in the time of Jesus and his disciples. Jewish tradition first tells of scribes who perform miracles from the period

around A.D. 70 onwards and especially in the second and subsequent centuries. So most of these stories of miracles are further
removed from the events they describe than are those of the
Gospels. But as in previous centuries, the Jews of the first century
A.D. naturally kept alive by scripture reading, public worship, and
prayers the memory of the great acts of God, and of miracle
workers like Moses, Elijah, and Elisha in particular. And, as can
be seen from the appearance of the so-called messianic prophets,
it was expected that the time of salvation would see a renewal of
the miracles of the wilderness and the arrival of a prophet like
Moses, in fact of a new Moses.

But the Hellenistic world also had its miracles. Here special
people like magicians and priests, philosophers and poets, generals
and lawgivers, and above all kings and rulers, were generally
looked on as embodiments of divine power, as "men of god", who
therefore joined the world of the gods when they died and became
revered in cults of their own as heroes and as special benefactors
and saviours. A man of forceful personality who towered above
ordinary people in knowledge and power was regarded as a revelation of divine power, as a *theios anēr*, a "divine man". The Hellenistic world celebrated as miracle workers "men of god" like Apollonius of Tyana and, still more, gods like the famous god of
healing, Aesculapius, whose miraculous cures and divers miracles
are praised in the temple inscriptions preserved at Epidaurus and
Rome.

When therefore we consider the character of the tradition of
miracles and the literary classification of miracle narratives, it is
not at all surprising that many miracle stories in the Gospels, particularly the healing pericopes, display sometimes stereotyped characteristics which are also found in the miracle stories of the ancient
world. The extent of this similarity, which may in part have been
the natural outcome of catechetical needs, must not however be
overestimated, as a comparison particularly with the far more
schematic inscriptions of Epidaurus has shown. It only establishes
after all a certain similarity in the technique of story-telling and
in the theme of miracle stories. But the similarity between Jewish,
Hellenistic, and early Christian miracle stories did long ago raise
the further question of whether there is not a much more fundamental connection. Do not these miracle stories suggest that there
was a basically similar primitive stage of religious thinking char-

acterized by a fondness for miracle, which was ready to attribute
particularly remarkable phenomena, which we today explain quite
naturally (things like epilepsy, dumbness, or raving madness), to
supernatural, divine, or demonic forces? Could the Jewish and
Gentile-Hellenistic tradition of miracle stories, particularly the Hellenistic concept of the "man of god", have contributed substan-
tially to a subsequent over-painting of the figure of Jesus, once his
adherents had proclaimed that this Jesus was the Son of God and
Saviour who had now appeared on earth? Could it be that in the
propagation of the Christian faith "exorcisms" and other spontaneous healings by Jesus, which today would be regarded as
psychosomatic cures, came to be understood and represented as
real miracles, so as to demonstrate and illustrate the fullness of
divine power in their "sōtēr", saviour, their redeemer-god? It is
impossible to answer these questions fairly with a general "Yes"
or "No".

We cannot simply say "Yes" because there is no doubt that
from the standpoint of the history of religion, when considered as
a whole, the miracle stories of the Gospels do have a striking
quality of uniqueness. Unlike them most of the rabbinic miracle
stories, for example, are obviously sheer invention, despite certain
points of contact with history. Their historical details are totally
unreliable, and they merely illustrate certain points of rabbinic
teaching with obviously apologetic tales, showing for instance how
a good deed is rewarded or lauding the great knowledge and piety
of a rabbi or even the unimpeachable honour of the God of Israel,
as in the very many punishment miracles. A further characteristic of
these Jewish miracle stories, which as we have said are much
later in time, is the frequent occurrence of distinctly spectacular
and bizarre features, so that, for example, a supposed raising from
the dead is degraded to a malicious trick. And perhaps more
striking still, the supposed miracles such as healings, raisings of
the dead, and punishment miracles are regarded as answers to
prayer or else as the results of occult knowledge and complicated
magical practices. This can be seen particularly in charms uttered
over the sick-bed and in exorcisms.

If we turn to the Gentile world of Hellenism, the dedicatory
inscriptions at Epidaurus, mentioned before, ascribe most of the
miracles, such as various sorts of healings, extremely generous
cures of all kinds of mishaps, raisings from the dead, the gift of

children, sometimes meeting the wish for a boy or girl as desired, as well as other really strange miracles, to a dream experience in the temple, in which the god Aesculapius performs operations which are sometimes grotesque, such as cutting off a head to remove a tapeworm and then successfully replacing the head. Even in those cases where the god does not himself appear his help is obviously regarded as a magical intervention. Healings and cures are effected by the footstep of the god or of his horses, by the bite of his sacred geese, or the lick of snakes and dogs. Not least important, as is shown by the major role which payment occupies, is the business of raising the necessary cash for the maintenance of the facilities at Epidaurus, as well, of course, as the matter of preserving inviolate the prestige of the god, defilement of which results in all sorts of dreadful punishment miracles.

There can be no doubt that there is a great gulf between these non-Christian miracle stories and those of the Gospels. The Gospels have no apologetic stories of the rabbinic kind, no miracles of reward, payment, or profit. Jesus himself did not perform any miracles for ostentation or for punishment. It is characteristic of the Jesus of the Gospels that he does not perform every outlandish and spectacular miracle possible. He cannot be made to be a mere wonder-worker either by his unbelieving opponents or by the people who seek his material help. We hear nothing of the various sorts of demons with their fantastic names and hierarchies, nor of places and times which are particularly exposed to demons, as in the bizarre, common stories of exorcisms. The Jesus of the Gospels does meet people who are possessed, people that is who, according to the ideas of the time, were victims of demons, but he never for instance meets demons roaming around on their own. None of the miracles occurs during sleep, and not one of them even depends solely on the efficacy of the prayer of Jesus. Both harsh treatment and surgical operations are foreign to him. There are practices which are reminiscent of magic, but these are exceptions and will be dealt with later. Even when Jesus touches sick people with his hand or takes hold of them, with (or occasionally without) a word of command, the tradition leaves no doubt that it regards the will of Jesus, revealed in such an action and most of all in the word he speaks, as the real power working the miracle. The absolute conviction with which the tradition shows Jesus performing mighty acts also accords with this, whereas the later, rationalizing biography of Apollonius significantly makes its hero out to be merely an outstanding savant and diagnostician so as to save him from the charge of being a magician. What this comparison between the miracle stories of the Gospels and those of the contemporary world around shows is the extremely striking originality and distinct superiority of the miracle-worker of the Gospels, despite the relationship in narrative technique and subject matter. And this needs to be explained.

Of course nowadays all the miracle stories in the Gospels, like miracles in general, are regarded as incredible in themselves, and the more they override what we normally experience and find inexplicable the more incredible they become. But to say this in no way provides an explanation of the distinct originality and purpose of the miracle stories of the Gospels, for they cannot all be understood and disposed of simply as instances of miracles borrowed from the world around.

We are justified, then, methodologically and factually in turning our attention to the unique correlation of event and meaning which the Gospels or Jesus himself claim for his "mighty acts", as the early Church called the miracles. And this eschatological correlation of meaning is certainly original, as compared both with the miracle stories of Judaism and Hellenism and more significantly with every sort of messianic expectation held by the Jews. The double expression "hearing and seeing", which is not found in the Old Testament but is undoubtedly a genuine feature of significance for Jesus' message, also points to the eschatological significance of the present. That Jesus did perform "mighty acts"—no matter for the time being how many and which of the "miracles" of the Gospels do come into this category—may be taken to be significant to the extent that Jesus made the claim to be bringing in the redemptive act of God, promised for the last days, by his action here and now; to the extent that he himself regarded the mighty acts performed by himself as warning signs of the reign of God breaking in, which fulfilled and confirmed the prophecies of redemption; to the extent, in fact, that he himself characterized these acts as the clearest and most compelling manifestation of the action of God, promised of the last days but beginning now in his ministry. So whether we really believe in and acknowledge as original the miraculous acts of Jesus depends finally on whether we acknowledge the "miracle"—if I may so put it—behind these

8

miraculous acts; whether, that is, we allow the Jesus of history to make a unique redemptive claim for his present ministry *and*, I must add, we are willing to accept it. For however emphatically the Jesus of the Gospels stresses the revelatory, symbolic, and authenticating power of his mighty acts, he certainly does not see in them empirical proof which satisfies him and which might to some extent logically compel belief in the revelation of God which begins in him. In accordance with Jesus' own understanding it is not really open to us to argue that, since Jesus does things which cannot be explained according to the laws and forces of nature known to us (or which can only be thought of as exceptions and so cannot in fact be taken into account), therefore he is the absolute, final revealer and redeemer—God himself indeed, just as necessarily and self-evidently as $2 \times 2 = 4$. Despite their evidential force, the mighty acts of Jesus are the object of faith on the same basis as his words about the breaking-in of God's rule which accompany them and interpret them. As with his proclamation in word, the proclamation in action made by his miracles is also always essentially an address from God, an offer of salvation. It is an act and gift of God in which he graciously turns to man and thereby encourages man to turn personally to him. That is, it urges a man to "conversion", as Jesus understood it, in which a man is totally committed.

It is highly striking then that the miracle-worker of the Gospels breaks right through, and goes beyond, the categories and limits of thought of the Jewish and Gentile world at decisive points. Nevertheless it is equally impossible to answer the question we posed at the beginning about the connection between the miracle pericopes in the Gospels and pre-Christian and non-Christian miracle stories and motifs with an unqualified no. The comparison with the "miracles" of the Jewish and Hellenistic world has enabled scholars to see not only how unique and markedly original was the style of the Gospel miracle-worker; it has at the same time opened their eyes also to characteristics which are distinctly Jewish or Hellenistic and which make the miracle stories of the Gospels very much like those of the world around. Moreover the character and purpose of the Gospel traditions about Jesus leave room for questions about the character and scope of the miracles of Jesus. Or, to put it another way, they leave room for the possibility that the actual needs of preaching and catechetical teaching caused them here and there to pick up characteristics and elements from non-Christian miracle stories. In fact it is possible that, following Old Testament analogies and motifs, they particularly made use of essentially "kerygmatic" miracle stories. Again, we must confine ourselves to a few suggestions.

In all likelihood the cursing of the fig tree was originally a parable which catechetical needs turned into a demonstration of the divine power of Jesus. It thus became a punishment miracle which was a highly important and recurrent feature of the miracle tradition of Judaism and Hellenism. So also, two units originally handed down separately have been joined together to become in Mark 2 a distinctive miracle of testimony and demonstration which, in the form we have it, establishes in a way that can be checked Jesus' power to forgive sins. At least some element of contemporary healing techniques, which were also techniques practised by the early Church, has crept into the presentation of those particularly striking actions which go beyond gestures of the hand to involve the use of spittle, as especially with the healing in stages of the blind man in Mark 8.22–6 and parallels. Perhaps this is also due to the particular importance which was attached in Church teaching to the symbolic meaning of the healing of the blind and of the deaf and dumb, which already existed in the Old Testament and late Judaism. The story of the woman with a haemorrhage, who expects to be healed merely by touching Jesus' robe and is healed by power issuing from Jesus, makes use of the well-known idea of "mana". Commentators today are thus quite right not to be really concerned with questions of why, in the Gerasene pericope of Mark, Jesus gets involved in disputes with demons, why this once he forces them to disclose their names, and in particular why in this case he should have demonstrated the breaking-in of God's reign at such cost to the owners and to the animal world—there were after all about 2000 swine—without the slightest explanation or justification or even a hint of sympathy. A catechist may well have taken features of a Jewish story of demons being driven out in a Gentile area and used them as an impressive illustration for his hearers of the incomparable superiority of Jesus over the concentrated forces which ruin life. But the very fact that this Gerasene pericope is such an exception confirms how unique the exorcisms of Jesus are, for in contrast to Jewish exorcisms they are not carried out by name-magic nor do they require a spectacular demonstration with highly dubious after-effects.

But the Gospels do include a type of miracle story which cannot really be regarded as a manifestation of the reign of God breaking in. They claim to be explicit proofs of the messiahship of Jesus, of his status as bearer of salvation, or else they set out to prove a divine authority of Jesus which encompasses both life and death, to demonstrate a revelation of the divine which has now become available to all. For some time now scholars have been arguing whether miracle-stories of this kind were originally intended to give an account of what Jesus actually did on specific occasions or whether they were really intended to state and proclaim who and what Jesus is. And they have not pursued this argument—or at least they should not have done—on the ground that in the story of Jesus, as in any other story, nature miracles have to be ruled out *a priori* and on principle. The important considerations have arisen from the texts themselves. Quite apart from questions of fact and difficulties of internal criticism which in certain miracle-stories militate against any attempt to read off history from them, a glance at the style of particular miracle-stories, at the intention behind them which shaped their content and construction, and at the Old Testament parallels and motifs, has forced scholars to ask this question: Why should the need to give illustrations in preaching and catechesis not have led the early Christians to use, for instance, the feeding miracles of the Old Testament, when they wanted by means of an even greater feeding miracle to present Jesus as the fulfilment of past history who excels all the prophets, when they wanted to show him as the second Moses and shepherd of the last days, which according to his own words he intended to be? And what would be the significance of the early Church in its preaching representing Jesus in kerygmatic miracle-stories as like Yahweh himself "who tramples the waves of the sea" (Job 9.8), who stills "the roaring of the seas, the roaring of their waves..." (Psalm 65.7)? It would be quite wrong and inappropriate to talk in this case of invention or falsification or of a myth or anything of the sort. Following on the claim made by Jesus that in his ministry God's activity promised for the last days was beginning and being made manifest, the early Church might simply have found it necessary to use an extremely telling style in order to conduct their mission among contemporary ideas, in order to express who really was the one and only *theios anēr*, the "man of god", the revelation, the demonstration and manifestation of the divine in this world; the one whom they proclaimed "Kyrios Jesus Christos"—that is, the Christ, Jesus, who is Lord, the divine Lord.

12 The Lord's Supper: Concepts and Developments

WILLI MARXSEN

If we want to know what is the meaning of the Christian Lord's Supper we naturally turn to the New Testament for an answer. This seems appropriate, for it is *Jesus'* supper which the Church still intends to celebrate. But this very intention raises problems for any direct reference to the New Testament. This is clear from linguistic considerations alone. The Supper originated in the Palestinian world where Aramaic was spoken, which is a late form of Hebrew. But the New Testament has come down to us in Greek. So what we have is in translation. This is not to say that the twenty-seven writings collected together in the New Testament were originally written in Aramaic and then translated into Greek. As we now have them, they were composed by men who had a command of Greek and wrote directly in Greek. But this is what aggravates our problem. For if we ask today what is the meaning of the Christian Lord's Supper and look at the New Testament, we get an answer which, because it was composed in Greek, is also framed more or less in Greek categories of thought. If we want to know what the Supper was like in the beginning, we need to work back behind the existing text. But can this be done if (except for certain formula-type phrases) there never was an Aramaic text behind the Greek text which we can reconstruct, but a "set of circumstances", a custom, just a meal, for us to identify? The attempt must at least be made.

We start however from linguistic considerations with the problem of translation. You only need to know one foreign language to be aware of the difficulties of translation. Only rarely is it possible to translate word for word. You have rather to grasp as a whole the meaning of what the one language expresses and then rephrase it in the other language (again, as a whole). So translation, if it is done properly, is always a process of creation as well. If this is true of languages which are related to each other, it is even more true of languages which belong to quite different families— as is the position in our case where we have Hebrew and Aramaic, which are Semitic languages, and Greek, which is of Indo-European origin. This can be demonstrated for instance by the forms of the verb, which cannot really be compared with each other at all. Greek, just like our own language, has distinct forms of the perfect, imperfect, present, future, etc. In Hebrew it is completely different. There is no present; but neither are there any proper tenses at all. Hebrew thinks solely in terms of process, and states whether the process was concluded in the past (or just now) or whether it has not yet been concluded. In the first case the perfect, as it is called, is used; in the other case the imperfect. There are no other forms which express time.

This grammatical difference in itself creates considerable difficulties for the translator. Which of the many forms of the verb in his own language should he use in a particular case? Often only the context can decide. But the problem goes much deeper than this. For what we are up against here is a certain limitation to the possibility of translation at all. No language was conceived on a drawing board and then handed out to the various peoples for use. Every language is an expression of the thinking, experience, and feeling of a particular people at a particular time. While thought and feeling are implanted in a child by the process of learning a language, it is with the help of this language that he later expresses this thought and feeling. We can only really understand the difference between Hebrew and Greek (and of course between Hebrew and our language too) if we are clear in our own minds about this connection between speech and thinking and experience. We can see this for ourselves in one or two aspects of the Israelite cult which are closely connected with these strange forms of the Hebrew verb. The origin of most of the cultic festivals of Israel can no longer be determined with any real certainty. For the most part they were originally nature festivals, or else they were taken over from religions round about. But the significant thing is that they were all thoroughly "historicized"—or, to put it more clearly, they were attached in a very striking way to events of the past.

Let me give one or two examples. Before the settlement, the Feast of the Passover was celebrated in spring by individual tribes which were still nomadic, just before moving on to new pastures (i.e. on the point of departure). Later, this departure was connected with the Exodus from Egypt, in "remembrance" of which the festival was now celebrated. The Mazzoth Festival (the Feast of Unleavened Bread) was also linked with the Exodus. Later, the Feast of Tabernacles (originally the festival of the autumn vintage) was used as the "remembrance" of various events in the history of Yahweh's dealings with his people. The Feast of Weeks was linked up with the making of the covenant on Sinai. The Feast of Purim (probably of pagan origin) came to be celebrated in the post-exilic period as the "remembrance" of how the Jews' enemies were slain at the time of Xerxes, that is as the "remembrance" of the preservation of God's people.

I have put the word "remembrance" in inverted commas because we shall misunderstand the nature of these festivals if we think in terms of a *memorial* of the Exodus from Egypt, a *memorial* of the great acts of Yahweh, a *memorial* of the preservation of Israel. It is much more true to say that these saving events were "recalled". The distinctive feature of these "remembrances" is that the time-gap was, as it were, nullified, and these events of the past were now conceived of not as happenings cut off in the past but as experiences shared in the present. Thus an old instruction of the second century A.D. says that "It is the duty of every generation to think of itself as if it had personally come up out of Egypt". The individual elements of the meal also then came to be interpreted in this way. Bitter herbs were now eaten because the Egyptians had made life bitter for the Israelites' forefathers; unleavened bread was now eaten because their forefathers had had no time at the Exodus to wait for dough to be leavened; and at the Feast of Tabernacles booths were now built and lived in because their forefathers had lived in booths on the journey through the wilderness. An indication of how much the past was brought home within Jewish thinking about time—it would be better to say, within Jewish experience of time—is given by the ordering of the Passover Feast as preserved and practised by the small group of Samaritans right into this century. The participants at the meal are girded, carry a staff in the hand, and eat up the lamb in great haste, for they *are* about to leave Egypt. It is very difficult for us to conceive of this way of re-presenting the past; and it is unlikely that we shall be able to achieve it completely.

Corresponding to this re-presentation is an anticipation, for the festivals, as they are now celebrated, are also eschatological festivals. This relationship with the future is, for instance, expressed in the words of the Passover liturgy: "This year here, next year in the land of Israel; this year slaves, next year free men." Another sentence runs: "Grant, O Yahweh our God, the God of our forefathers, that we may live to celebrate the festivals, *coming to meet us* peacefully . . . and that we may eat there of the festive sacrifices and of the Passover sacrifice." The Passover Feast was a high feast of messianic expectation. But the same can also be said of the Feast of Tabernacles. In the Book of Zechariah (14.16), the last days are described in these terms: "Then every one that survives of all the nations that have come against Jerusalem shall go up year after year to worship the King, the Lord of hosts, and to keep the feast of booths." Within a pattern of ideas like these we can see how the last days could come to be thought of as a meal at the table of Yahweh. This eschatological meal came to *meet* those who now reclined at the table. They were already celebrating it as the future now breaking in on them. It is of course taken for granted that every Jewish meal had a cultic character, that Jews were not allowed to have table fellowship with Gentiles, and that Jews who were ritually unclean were also not admitted to table. They ate before God, before the God who had made the covenant with their fathers and whose kingdom they were approaching. The meal mediated fellowship with Yahweh, but it mediated this fellowship historically. Or, to put it another way, the meal "recalls" or "remembers" Yahweh's redeeming presence, both past and future.

With these ideas as the background we can see what an unprecedented thing it was when Jesus invited sinners and taxcollectors to his table. This was not just ordinary human kindness. It was much more. Jesus reincorporated these people into the covenant with God, and here and now gave these very people whom strict Jews looked down on a share in the coming kingdom of God. This is an essential feature of the message of Jesus: he offers fellowship with God without attaching conditions which must first be fulfilled. Paul later expresses this as "justification of the sinner without the works of the law".

But now we must get back to the Lord's Supper. We know that
the primitive Church was meeting together for meals soon after
Easter. After what we have said this is not only understandable
but what we would expect. There was no Christian liturgy as yet.
But there was a Christian Church. How were they to find the form
of gathering appropriate to them? While the Church of Jerusalem
kept up (or resumed) a certain connection with the Temple, they
could not meet there as the Church. But then the gathering at the
common meal presented itself as the place where in any case fellowship with God and with one another was experienced in a
singular way. This custom which they had taken over had of course
now to be modified and filled with a new meaning. How this
came about can still be clearly seen at certain points. There is an
interesting indication at one point in the accounts of the institu-
tion of the Last Supper. In what is probably the oldest form, which
Paul hands on to us and which he quotes in 1 Corinthians 11, the
words over the bread and the cup do not, as in Mark 14, follow
straight on from one to the other but are separated by the meal.
The words over the cup are introduced by: "In the same way he
took the cup *after supper* . . .".

Here we come up against the problem we have already mentioned, the problem of translation. Our Greek texts do not go back
directly to an Aramaic original. They were put together in Greek
and allow us to see that, for reasons to be discussed later, the meal
proper was left out of the Lord's Supper in the Greek, Hellenistic
world. The form of celebration which is familiar to us has its
origin here. But the phrase "after supper" is a relic of the Palestinian period of the Lord's Supper and shows that at first the
Lord's Supper really was held as a full meal. Among the Jews the
festival meal began with the breaking of bread, over which grace
was said. Then followed the meal proper. At the end the cup of
blessing, as it was called, was circulated and over it was said the
thanksgiving. For our purposes it is the texts of these prayers
which are interesting. One thanksgiving which has come down to
us runs: "We thank thee, O Yahweh our God, that thou didst
give to our forefathers for an inheritance the pleasant, good and
broad land, that thou didst bring us out of the land of Egypt and
hast redeemed us from the house of bondage. . . ." Here then the
past is remembered or "recalled". But there is also a "recalling"
of the future. So for instance another thanksgiving ends with the

words: "May the merciful one make us worthy of the days of the Messiah and of the life of the world to come. . . ." After what we have said about the distinctive character of the Hebrew experience of time, it is quite clear that these prayers cannot be understood as intended to make those at the meal think *about* the past and *about* the future. Rather, the present meal is here linked with the redemptive past, and the redemptive future comes to meet those who take part in the meal. Those reclining at table are those who belong to the covenant.

It was precisely this situation which gave the early Church the opportunity to express with the help of a modification of the formularies in what capacity they were celebrating the Lord's Supper and how they understood it. This is still to be seen most clearly in the form of the words over the cup passed on by Paul: this cup is the new covenant in the blood of Jesus. We must note that there is no reference here to the contents of the cup. We easily read this in because it corresponds to our form of the celebration. But this idea is not in the text. In what way is the cup the covenant? Now it is not the cup as such but the cup as it circulates to which the words apply. The Church celebrating the meal, among which the cup circulates, is the Church of the new covenant. But this new covenant has its foundation in the blood of Jesus, that is, in the sacrificial death of Jesus. This is a new covenant which has abrogated the old covenant. This new covenant, which God has made in and through Jesus, is "recalled" at the Lord's Supper. The words over the bread must then also be understood in the same way. The bread is broken by the head of the house and then handed round, and the words "This is my body" said. We cannot be sure what were the words used at this point in the Jerusalem supper. The word "body" is a Greek sort of expression which however has an ecclesiological connotation; that is, it designates the Church. Body here means the body of Christ in the sense that Christ and his own are united in one concept. So here too, then, the motif of remembrance lies behind the words of interpretation. The people celebrating the meal, among whom the bread circulates, are the actual community who "recall" Jesus. We can now take up again a point made already. I drew attention to the meals of the earthly Jesus, in which the distinctive character of his message and mission are expressed. When the early Church met at

112 JESUS IN HIS TIME

supper after Easter, they now "recalled" these very meals of Jesus, and what Jesus had offered them there became reality again.

Whether Jesus on the eve of his death expressly instituted the Lord's Supper cannot be adequately discussed in this context. From an historical point of view it is most improbable. But this does not mean that the Lord's Supper does not go back to Jesus at all. The meals of Jesus are after all remembered. But the question remains why the origin of the Supper was, as it were, given a date. What happened here is something quite similar to what we saw going on in the development of the Jewish festivals: what were originally nature festivals were brought into connection with Yahweh's dealings with his people. They wanted to "recall" these redemptive actions. So the early Church, which at first "recalled" the meals of the earthly Jesus in their supper, connected it later with the Passion of Jesus, because they saw in the cross the decisive redemptive act of God.

But now we must look at the remembrance from the other direction. The early Church expected the *parousia*, i.e. the second coming of Jesus, to break in very shortly; and they now gave expression to this idea in their prayers at table. The words passed on by Paul in connection with the tradition of the Lord's Supper are illuminating on this point; "... until he comes". Even more interesting is a liturgical term which occurs twice in the New Testament (once in fact in Aramaic) which was almost certainly originally to be found in the celebration of the Lord's Supper: *maranatha* —Come, Lord (or in the other occurrence: Come, Lord Jesus). There has been much argument among scholars whether the primitive Church was praying here for Jesus to come *to the celebration of the Supper* or whether they were looking to the coming of Jesus *in the last days*, that is, whether the prayer was for the *parousia* to come soon. Thinking in these alternatives is a typically western approach. It presupposes our way of thinking about time. We are almost incapable of talking in terms other than of an either/or. But what we regard as alternatives in our thinking about time was regarded by the Hebrews in their experience of time as a unity. The early Church knew that they were living after the time of Jesus. But they still celebrated his meals; they "recalled" them by re-presentation. The early Church knew too that the *parousia* of Jesus was still to come. But Jesus still came to meet them at the Supper; they "recalled" his coming by anticipation.

Was it possible to express this in Greek? It is obvious that such an idea could not have been translated word for word. It was necessary to get a grasp of the whole in order to reformulate it as a whole in a new linguistic and conceptual framework. But this did not come about as the result of a deliberate, and therefore single, process of translation, but by a long development. For this reason we cannot here and now give a summary of the concepts of the Supper which existed in Hellenistic Christianity but must be content to try and elucidate one or two stages in the process of translation so that we can appreciate the new forms of expression associated with it.

The Jews of the *diaspora* (i.e. the Jews not living in Palestine) were for the most part bilingual at the time of Jesus. The tradition of the Lord's Supper handed on by Paul was probably formulated in Antioch where, as far as we can tell, the first Christian Church outside Palestine was formed. In that tradition we can see alongside the original Jewish elements (such as: "after supper", and the connection of the circulation of the cup with the covenant) the Hellenistic Greek element as well, to which I have already referred (the linking of the broken bread, as it circulates, with the body of Christ). We then see the next stage in Mark. The phrase "after supper" is omitted there. So the words spoken at the breaking of the bread connect with those said over the cup. This must be done intentionally. But it is illuminating to see how the words said over the cup are here completely recast. In Mark they run: "This is my blood of the covenant, which is poured out for many" (14.24). The focus here is on the *contents* of the cup, and so it becomes evident that we have here a quite different understanding of the Supper. At the Palestinian Supper the words over the bread and the cup applied to the *whole* meal. At these two points it was the practice to state the meaning of the whole Supper. But now these words become attached to the individual actions and refer to the bread and the wine. The food comes to be consumed as the body and blood of Christ. This decisive recasting of the Lord's Supper is connected with Hellenistic ideas. According to these, communication of the "divine" to man is always conceived of in material terms. Even "spirit" in Hellenistic thinking is an extremely refined substance. So when the Lord's Supper was celebrated in the Greek world, Christ came to his own in the sacred food, in the bread and the wine. There was no longer any meaning in a meal

translate not the understanding of meal itself
(which would be impossible) but what it conveys.
salvation

114   JESUS IN HIS TIME

between receiving the bread and the wine, so it dropped out. But because the memory lingered on until much later that the Church in earlier times had held a full meal, in many places there grew up, as well as the sacramental Lord's Supper, *agapes*, as they were called, love feasts which were purely fellowship meals.

It can be seen then that the Lord's Supper was "translated". The question which we must finally ask is: Was the translation successful? Let us be quite clear about one thing. Without translation it would not have been possible to celebrate the Lord's Supper at all in the Greek world. Translation was a necessity. But what was to be translated? To say "a meal" is not good enough, for it was just not feasible that a Jewish custom should be naturalized among Greek Christians. That would only have been possible if at the same time the Jewish experience of time could have been transmitted to the Greeks. Then in effect only Jews could have become Christians, and Greeks would have had to become Jews in order to become Christians. But if we say that it was what the meal conveyed which needed translating—the salvation which had broken in in Jesus and which was "recalled" in the meal—then the translation may be said to have been a success to some extent, for a Greek could not think of and experience the transmission of salvation historically, but only materially, and that means through the food.

We do indeed have to point out the limits of this, as of every translation. It cannot and must not take the place of the original. But this has unfortunately happened all too often. The controversies in the history of the Church up to our own day about the Lord's Supper have not infrequently originated precisely in the fact that the original was not taken into consideration. It is as little possible now to get inside the material ideas of the Hellenist with his holy food as it was to get inside the Jewish meal at the first translation. What had to be done then was that a translation be made of what the meal conveyed. And so now too a real translation has to have in mind what needs to be conveyed. If the agent of this transmission could be changed in New Testament times, there is no reason why this should not be possible now too. If we can see how this first process of translation was carried out, it may be a help to us in making our translation. For this translation of the Lord's Supper always needs doing over and over again.

13 Problems of Legal History in the Gospels

DIETER NÖRR

I begin with an example, the story of the adulteress in John's Gospel (8.3ff). The Pharisees and scribes appear with the adulteress before Jesus and say: "Master, this woman has been caught in the very act of adultery. Now in the law, Moses commanded us to stone such. What do you say?" This question was aimed at drawing Jesus into the conflict between the Mosaic law and his teaching. As you know, Jesus avoided making a direct decision by saying, "Let him who is without sin among you be the first to throw a stone at her." At this, the accusers left the woman, and Jesus sent her away with the warning to sin no more.

A lawyer might approach this text in two ways. On the one hand he could ask what help the story gives in settling legal problems today, and on the other what information it yields for the history of the law. The former approach would require not only fundamental sympathy with the idea of a Christian legal system but would also lead on to the current dispute about what is just law, or to be more precise, about whether, for instance, adultery is a punishable offence. I do not intend to pursue this angle here, interesting though the discussion would be. We shall be concerned only with the historical question of the legal system which forms the background of the story.

A proper answer to this question would require our going thoroughly into the juridical and social problems of the ancient world. We would need to have a look at the Jewish view of marriage, and from this we would have to establish not only in what way adultery was culpable but also the reasons for the particular form of punishment. For the penalty was not enforced by the husband as a matter of personal revenge, as would perhaps have accorded with the viewpoint of a strongly patriarchal society. In fact, the husband does not enter into the matter at all; it is the people who carry out the execution. Moreover, the fact that the penalty is enforced not by an executioner but by the people would lead us to ask how the Jews understood the penalty. For this we would need to draw on other oriental legal systems for comparison. They would then have to be examined to see whether execution by the people is peculiar to the Jews.

It is my intention here to proceed more simply. According to Mosaic law (e.g. Deut. 22.22), adulterers are punished with death. The way the sentence is to be carried out is not laid down there. But from the prophet Ezekiel (16.40) as well as from the penalty for breach of promise (Deut. 22.24), it appears that the death penalty was carried out by stoning. Thus we arrive at an old Jewish legal principle, to which our story refers: adulterers are stoned. But was this legal principle still in force at the time of Jesus or, if we extend the period a little, in the years of the first Roman emperors? The answer we give to this question could decide the authority we should allow to the text of the Gospel at this point.

Two difficulties crop up here which cannot be solved with any real certainty but only hypothetically. The one arises from a comparison with the Mishnah (Sanhedrin 7.4). The Mishnah gives an interpretation of the Torah, the Mosaic law, in modernized terms: without it the Mosaic law could no longer have been applied because of completely changed social and economic conditions. Essentially it dates from roughly the same period as the Gospels and it probably reached its final shape in the second half of the second century A.D. According to the Mishnah (for reasons which are not of interest here) adultery is punishable not by stoning but, except in special cases, by strangulation. In Jewish thinking this was a milder form of death sentence. If then we want to harmonize the text of John's Gospel with historical fact, two possibilities arise. Either, at the time when John's Gospel originated, stoning of an adulteress was still the law and the change in form of execution had not yet gained acceptance, or else it was illegal and, as is attested in similar cases (Sanhedrin 7.2), carried out through ignorance.

More serious is another difficulty which our passage shares with the principal legal problem of the Gospels—the trial of Jesus.

According to John's Gospel (18.28f), Jesus was handed over to the governor Pontius Pilate because the Jewish courts did not have capital powers and so could not pass sentence of death upon him. In the story of the adulteress, on the other hand, there is no mention of the Roman authorities having to be brought in. Moreover the evidence of the sources is contradictory. One part tells in favour of a capital jurisdiction of the Romans only, other sources have the Jews exercising the death penalty. This matter of the Romans' capital jurisdiction brings us into the thick of a controversy which oddly enough takes problems of religion and history into the realm of formal jurisprudence, and has passionately excited theologians and laymen, Jews and Christians for centuries —the controversy over the legality or illegality of the proceedings against Jesus. The legal historian is inclined on the whole to affirm at least the technical legality of the proceedings. But I am not going to enter into the details of the trial of Jesus here. Rather I intend to confine myself to a brief consideration of the capital jurisdiction of the Romans.

If one set of authorities supports and another denies the capital jurisdiction of the Romans and if there is no reason at all to suggest that one set is false, then only a qualified answer is possible. In this case only two possibilities need to be discussed. On the one hand it is conceivable that the Roman authorities in principle reserved the death penalty to themselves, but in cases of no political consequence, among which adultery belonged, they acquiesced in the Jews' exercising the death penalty. This would accord with what we know of the undogmatic way in which the Romans ruled. They were keen on preserving the old institutions and traditions of their subjects. On the other hand, the contradiction in the evidence could also be explained by an old legal principle for which there is also evidence in other ancient codes. In those cases where the Jews exercised capital powers or, as in the story of the adulteress, sought to exercise them, the culprit was every time apparently caught in the act. The modern constitutional principle that no penalty can be imposed without the verdict of a court of law cannot simply be projected back into the past. In the context of a naturalistic view of justice, the proceedings and verdict of a court of law are superfluous when someone is caught in the act. Because the act is plain to all, the punishment can be carried out there and then. This way of carrying out a sentence should not be regarded,

9

as it often is, as lynch law. For it is based on a legal procedure in which, as we might put it, the deed passes sentence on the doer. Consequently, it could be that the Romans' reservation on capital jurisdiction held only for genuine trials but not for summary proceedings where someone was caught in the act.

This discussion of a passage which at first sight does not seem to place great demand on legal scholarship, illustrates the point that theological exposition cannot ignore the legal background if it aims to do more than allegorize or moralize. The stories and parables of the Gospels are shot through with legal problems far more than the modern reader of the Gospels would imagine. They crop up in contexts which appear as far removed from the law as the last words of Jesus from the cross in John's Gospel (19.26f), the parable of the Good Shepherd (John 10.11f), and the passages about the forgiveness of sins (for instance, Matthew 6.12; 18.23ff), to give only a few examples. Behind them lies not only the close connection of law and religion, so characteristic of Judaism, which makes the individual's relationship with God a legal relationship; they also indicate the almost intimate familiarity which men in the ancient world had with the legal system which applied to them, a familiarity which is characteristic of comparatively simple legal systems but would be utopian for us today.

But the legal approach to the Gospels not only has the purpose of assisting our theological and religio-historical understanding of the Gospels. It also helps us to investigate the legal system of the ancient world and as such is an end in itself. The elucidation of the legal background provides material for the exegesis of the text. More than that, it establishes how historically reliable the text is. But at the same time, the argument being inevitably circular in interpretation, the text itself becomes a source of information for the law which was in force in the Roman empire in the time of the Caesars. It is this second aspect that I now intend to consider briefly.

In our juridical approach to the story of the adulteress, we have already had to draw on at least two different legal systems, Jewish law and Roman law, in order to set straight the legal problems at least. But we cannot leave it at that, with just two legal systems. A few years ago a series of legal documents in Hebrew, Aramaic, Greek, and Latin was found with other objects in the caves of Murabba'ât, about sixteen miles south-east of Jerusalem. The caves lie in the extremely inaccessible desert to the west of the Dead Sea. Evidently the remnants of the Jewish freedom-fighters had retreated there after rising at the time of Hadrian against the rule of Rome. The documents come for the greater part from the time of the revolt itself and from the years shortly before. So they go back to the period in which the Gospels originated. If we take the languages of the documents as an indication (though not a certain one) of the legal systems behind them, we have to distinguish between at least three legal systems relevant to Palestine—Roman, Greek, and Jewish—and this leaves open the question whether the last should not be further divided. But if several legal systems stand side by side in this way we have to ask which of them is really the law of the land.

Here we touch on a problem which is quite crucial, not only for the history of Palestine but also for the ancient world as a whole and which has still not been entirely resolved today. The modern lawyer holds to a principle which is usually designated by the slogan "the unity of the legal system". This postulates a complete, consistent legal system within a sphere of law like the State. It is true that any legal system is made up of various spheres with their own norms, but conflicts have to be resolved in principle either by establishing a different set of legal norms or by precise delineation of the facts of the case. Above all, the standards which are to be applied when different legal systems clash are also based on the law then in force in the states concerned.

The laws of the ancient world were completely different. Any direct application of ideas familiar to us, such as those of a legal system and of the "validity" of the law, is out of the question. Simplifying very much, we can perhaps lay down the following principles:

1. Originally there was a certain tendency to think of every individual as having a particular legal system which was, as it were, his from birth. Should he find himself outside the territory where this legal system was applied by the courts, either he was in theory without rights or else he was treated even in a foreign country according to the legal system which was his by birth. Consequently an Athenian in Egypt, for example, either had to be without rights or continue to live under Athenian law. Where a community was closely knit socially and economically this "personality principle",

as it is called, created considerable difficulty for those who came under different spheres of law. Moreover, a strong state authority which pressed in the direction of a unified legal system was inevitably hostile to the principle. The practical consequences of the personality principle as such, as well as of the limitations which were necessarily laid upon it—but without ever being clearly regulated—were a considerable uncertainty about the law.

2. The fixed law of the ancient world can perhaps be compared in part with modern legal axioms. But the situations specifically covered by laws represented a disproportionately small part of the area which we today expect the law to cover. Apart from legal axioms of a rather technical nature, law-making was generally resorted to only when legal uncertainty and social conflicts made it unavoidable.

3. By far the greatest number of situations susceptible to law was left to custom, habit, and tradition, which in part grew up independently and in part were derived from neighbouring peoples. These constituted a hotchpotch of possible norms, quite contradictory at times, out of which the necessary usage was extracted case by case. The application and further development of this mass of customs was the task of the judicial authorities, no matter what public office they also held. The result is that neither contemporaries nor later historians have always been in a position to determine with any real certainty what law was in force at any particular time.

With these preliminaries, let us turn back to the Gospels. We are concerned here with the question of what type of law they indicate for the area of Palestine. For us to find the right approach for an answer to this, we must first discuss briefly which sorts of law we can expect in this area. In the first place, of course, we must mention Jewish law. It was based on the Torah, the Mosaic law, tailored in the Mishnah to changed circumstances and completed in the Talmud in late classical times. The Jewish law is in fact not only one of the best attested but also one of the most important legal creations of antiquity.

But the Jewish law did not develop in isolation. From its first beginnings Jewish culture was in constant interaction with the surrounding eastern world. A legal system which was intended to cover not only the internal affairs of the Jews but also their relations with non-Jews was bound to be influenced by other oriental legal systems. I am referring here to oriental legal systems in general as operative factors, for it has not yet been possible to distinguish at all adequately the influence of the particular legal systems of the surrounding eastern world. That borrowings did occur, above all from Babylonian law which was the commercial law of the Ancient Near East, may be taken as certain; but the nature and circumstances of these borrowings are uncertain. In general it can only be said that we can more readily expect such influences the nearer we move into those realms of law which have to do with commercial affairs. To give an example, business law is more open to influence than marriage law.

This maxim also holds good for the influence exerted by Greek law which in the Hellenistic period was strongly formative in the development of a uniform commercial law in the eastern Mediterranean. As the reaction against things Greek itself shows, Judaism was compelled to reckon with Greek culture. Despite all the struggles for independence, Palestine always came again under the sway of Hellenistic monarchies. Hellenized cities surrounded the country, Greek soldiers and merchants were always in evidence. The best indications of Greek influence on the law are the Greek deeds, of which the latest specimens date from the time of the Arab conquest of Palestine. And Greek influence was not confined to external affairs alone, for Greek deeds were used not only in business with foreigners but also in the internal business of the local population.

The last type of law which should be mentioned is Roman law. I shall not here consider the period of the later emperors when Roman law penetrated deeply into the legal life of the eastern provinces. With this exception, the sources show that the influence of Rome was limited essentially to the relationship of the Jewish subjects to the Roman authorities, that is, in modern terms, to public law. The principle still held good of not interfering in the internal affairs of their subject peoples, with the consequence that the old law remained essentially in being. But although the Romans allowed the Jews to keep a measure of self-government, even after the destruction of Jerusalem, the Roman governor still continued to be the highest judge in the land. His jurisdiction meant that it was possible for Rome to have a permanent influence on the law in force in Palestine.

Originally, then, we have Jewish law, oriental laws, Greek and Roman law; it is these four factors which made up the legal system in force in the world of Palestine. The weight which each of these factors carried was of course extremely varied. How do the Gospels stand as legal sources in relation to them?

As we would expect, Roman influence can be established only in the realm of public law. To give only two obvious examples, the general census in the empire which took Joseph and Mary to Bethlehem and the trial of Jesus before Pontius Pilate cannot be understood without some knowledge of the Roman system of taxation and Roman criminal law. But otherwise—and this is particularly the case with private law—there are no allusions to Roman law.

It is much more remarkable that in no passage can any borrowing of Greek legal concepts be established with certainty. Even in the realm of divorce (see Mark 10.11f) where Greek influence is generally alleged on the text of the Gospel at least, although it is very possible that we have Greek law, this is by no means proved. The Hellenization of eastern culture was not therefore necessarily matched by a thoroughgoing Hellenization of the legal system. But this point needs to be made more specific. What we could show is that Greek law and oriental law reached widely similar legal categories independently of each other. But as their development was essentially parallel, from the first there was little room for borrowings. In the eastern Mediterranean a measure of legal unity, which was very desirable from an economic and social point of view, could be widely achieved without mutual borrowings.

Roman legal institutions do not figure in the Gospels, apart from public law, and it cannot be proved that Greek legal institutions figure either. So, when we have instances of law in the Gospels with no parallels in Jewish law that we know of, we can conjecture that the influence comes from oriental law. It is true that we have to remember, as we have seen, that the official sources of Jewish law had already been shaped by the surrounding oriental world. But this conjecture of oriental influence can also be made only with reserve. Despite the wealth of Jewish legal sources, we cannot go on to deduce from them that all institutions in force in the Jewish legal world are mentioned in the written sources. Gaps in the tradition cannot simply be filled by conjectural borrowings. There are only a very few examples where the position of the sources generally allows us to believe that there were such borrow-ings.

We arrive then at the following conclusion. Essentially it is Jewish law which provides the background to the Gospels. From this in turn we can conclude that, in the Palestinian world from which the material of the Gospels may ultimately have originated, Jewish law was basically the law of the land despite Hellenistic influences and the Roman occupation. This plainly has implications for the historicity of the Gospels as well as for the cultural background to the ministry of Jesus. But this I am not competent to deal with, and must leave to the theologians and historians.

14 Forms of Religious Propaganda

DIETER GEORGI

What would the ordinary citizen of a Hellenistic city have been likely to think if he came across Christian missionaries like Philip, Barnabas, or Paul preaching at a street corner or in the market place? The answer is: nothing out of the ordinary. He might even have gone out into the street to hear preaching of this kind. What Acts chapter 17 says of the Athenians was true of the people of the Mediterranean world in general: "All the Athenians and the foreigners who lived there spent their time in nothing except telling or hearing something new" (17.21). This taste was met by a host of wandering preachers who propagated their various schemes of salvation in the streets and markets of the cities and also in the staging posts of the great highways. In doing this most of them had the explicit or implicit aim of reaching the world's capital, Rome, and of gaining a footing there for their message. This brings to mind the complaint made by the satirist Juvenal: "The Syrian Orontes [i.e. the river running through western Syria and flowing into the sea at Antioch, then the third largest city of the Roman empire] has long since been diverted into the Tiber."

Someone attending a synagogue would not find it unusual to be confronted with foreign Jews both before and during the service who quite as a matter of course took the floor in order to describe in their own way, sometimes a very singular way, the value and power of the Jewish religion and to give evidence of this. People particularly liked to go to the Jewish synagogue because of the variety of what went on there, and this variety reflected the broad-minded attitude shown in allowing wandering preachers to speak. It was no surprise then when a Paul appeared among them and began to preach. The only odd thing about Paul was that he was concerned not to attract attention in any way beyond this, for it was the aim of all wandering preachers and missionaries to attract attention, particularly in view of the great number of rivals that existed. In fact, this was almost their trademark. Each of them set out to demonstrate the exceptional character of his message by exceptional means. The assumption behind this intention of theirs was that there existed something like an international and inter-confessional scale of values for assessing the divine which made it possible for the public to weigh up what they were offering and assess the value of the message by the quality of the presentation. Missionaries as well as the public had something like a *lingua franca* and an international religious currency.

Within this medley of views the missionary had to demonstrate his capabilities as impressively as possible, so that the public could read off the degree of the divine competing for their attention in his particular religion or philosophy. The divine power exhibited in the performance of the messenger had to extend clearly into the realm of the supernatural, in knowledge of nature and the universe and in supreme mastery over the forces at work in these fields. Only in this way could the offer made by the particular form of propaganda carry any conviction, the offer of this particular scheme of salvation to change human fortune to eternal blessing, peace, and well-being. So the missionaries tended, because of their profession, to become "god-men". To this end they acquired from their traditions as long a list as possible of past heroes, equally able to perform miracles—in fact, the more the better. There was hardly any limit to fantasy in this field, but the purpose behind it was quite deliberate: to demonstrate the continuing spiritual and miraculous power of the particular religion or philosophy which they were championing.

The external appearance of the missionaries in itself was remarkable. For the most part they followed the example of the oldest missionaries in the Hellenistic world, the representatives of a popular philosophy which had grown out of a mixture of Cynic and Stoic ideas and traditions. These popular philosophers first attracted attention to themselves by begging. The philosopher Epictetus drew a neat caricature of this practice. He has someone say to himself who has decided on the vocation of the wandering preacher of philosophy: "I wear a rough cloak and I shall have one then; I have a hard bed even now and so I shall then; I shall take to myself a beggar's bag and a beggar's staff, and I shall begin to walk around and beg from those I meet, and revile them: and if I see someone who is clean-shaven or has a fancy hair-do or is dressed in scarlet, I will come down hard on him." Living by begging was not just the simplest way of supporting oneself while on the road. By this means a man could also demonstrate an interior greatness in himself which resulted in such obvious independence of society. But above all what he got out of begging was a wage, that is, remuneration for the spiritual power displayed in his manner of life, in his demeanour, and not least in his teaching, and for the salutary effect it had on the public. What the spiritual beggar got from his begging was meant to help him continue imparting his power without being hampered by the work-a-day world, and it was given for that purpose. Naturally, not everyone shared this view. There were mockers and critics enough, who saw in this begging, as in all the practices we will mention later, only deceit and greed, and in those who gave in faith only men who were weak and easily swindled. Since begging became the primary trademark of missionaries it is not surprising that we also find it much in evidence in the greatest missionary religion to precede Christianity, that is, in Judaism. Begging became almost proverbial in the environs of synagogues, simply because Jewish missionaries collected near synagogues in particular, and there too found temporary accommodation. Most of the Christian missionaries lived in the same fashion on the assistance offered by their particular public. A distinct exception to this again was Paul.

In addition to begging, however, the missionaries of the Hellenistic world had very different methods of attracting the attention of the multitude to the spiritual power at work in them and in their message. The miracles related in the New Testament represent only a few examples of practices which were widely common in the religious and philosophical propaganda of all beliefs. Driving out evil spirits from the possessed, i.e. the mentally ill, was just as common as miraculous healing of the lame, blind, and deaf, to give only a few examples. Even healings at a distance are recorded. The infertility of humans, animals, and fields could be remedied. Lost possessions as well as missing people could be located and recovered by the gift of clairvoyance, and men could

read minds and tell the stars and so foretell the future for themselves and for others. At this point we should mention the name
of one of Paul's contemporaries, Apollonius, because he was the
most famous of these missionaries and because his sphere of
activity was more or less the same as that of Paul. He came from
Tyana in Asia Minor, sixty-two miles north of Tarsus, the birth-
place of Paul, and he advocated a renewal of the philosophy of
Pythagoras in the sense of an enlightened religion and style of life,
which promised to give an inner-unity and perfection in the world.
Apollonius is alleged to have understood every language without
having learnt them, even the language of birds and animals, and
he also read people's minds. He foretold an epidemic of plague in
Ephesus as well as the assassination of the emperor Domitian, and
in both cases he was proved right. He even raised from the dead
a young girl who was already on the way to burial and gave her
back alive to her mourning bridegroom. Not only followers of
Apollonius but others too experienced appearances of the philosopher after his death and so claimed that he was immortal. It is
understandable that a message which could boast of such demon-
strations of divine power within it should be highly successful.

Of course, in all this as in the New Testament miracle stories we
are still faced with the question whether it all happened. There
are ample indications that belief in miracles and the tendency to
play up to it did lead to exaggerated legends and even to down-
right fraud. But on the other hand a public which expected sensational events of this sort as a matter of course and was at the same
time critical of them in view of the many rivals competing for
attention would not have been fobbed off all the time with mere
stories. The words from *Hamlet*, often used in defence of the
miracle stories of the New Testament, have to be allowed to apply
also to the miracle stories of the religions and philosophies which
were rivals to primitive Christianity: "There are more things in
heaven and earth than are dreamt of in your philosophy."

Alongside these sometimes sensation-mongering displays we
must not of course forget the capacity for rhetoric. It was one
of the most prominent and important divine gifts of the various
propagandists. After all the important thing was to clothe the
accomplishments of the deity concerned and those of his messengers
with the right words and present the particular scheme of salvation
in a vivid and compelling way, for they had to prove themselves

superior to a considerable group of rivals competing for the favour of the public. The readiness with which the popular philosophers picked an argument was generally feared; but precisely on this account their powerful style of speaking was readily imitated by other missionaries, not least by Jewish and Christian preachers.

The most important means of propaganda to which all the others were intended to lead, was of course worship, at least in so far as we are dealing with genuinely religious movements. Manifestations of divine power which had occurred outside the temples attracted the thankful and the curious into the consecrated buildings. Here they expected even clearer proofs of the value of the religion than those they had experienced outside. An essential method of arousing and capturing attention was to refer to secret practices which lay at the heart of the cult and which were revealed by degrees to those who were ready and prepared to learn them. The missionary religions of the Hellenistic world, for the most part eastern in origin, had not brought this type of mystery cult with them from the East but had encountered it among the Greeks and taken it over from them. These were the Greek mysteries, especially the Eleusinian mysteries. In these cults the mythical fate of the divinity was celebrated in dramatic secret ceremonies. It was only possible to participate in the cult by special membership of a kind of fraternity, which was conferred by initiation. But these mysteries, strange as it may sound, were for the most part communal institutions and were certainly celebrated to promote the good of the community. The idea was that from secrecy would flow, in rich abundance, springs for the salvation of the individual and for the well-being of all. But the mysteries had also soon made men realize that the fortunes of the individual were not only inseparable from those of the city-state but were also tied up with those of all mankind. So membership was even extended outside the ranks of the free citizens to those who were not free, and then even beyond the borders of the state to foreigners. This had happened most of all in the mysteries of Dionysus. They were the first Greek mystery cult to conduct a world-wide mission, to form mystery fraternities everywhere, and to keep them in some sort of contact with each other, not least by wandering preachers working as missionaries.

The eastern missionary religions took over practices and ideas from the mysteries in order to exploit the possibilities and advantages as well as the popular claim made by this model of organization, which had been proved in the Greek world. In this way it was possible for a cult to apply for the rights of a mystery fraternity with all the legal privileges and securities which went with it. The world-wide tendencies and successes which were to be seen in the mysteries provided examples for missionary activity which were worth imitating. But above all it was possible for a cult in this way to enter the competition for general significance and public influence. Such cults felt that they had a better claim than the Greek mysteries to promote the well-being of the individual as well as of mankind and to elevate it to the realm of the supernatural. The springs of religious power in the eastern religions flowed from mysterious depths. In Hellenistic thinking, however, the more mysterious a thing was the more divine it was. In time and space the heritage of the eastern missionary religions stretched back into deep obscurity. And according to the values which held good in Hellenism the older a thing was the closer it came to primeval times and so to the gods. Moreover, anything that came from the east had something of the basic quality of the rising sun. So the rule was that the older and more eastern a thing was, the truer it was. The oldest temples were in the east. In the east too were preserved mysterious traditions—mysterious not only because they were older, but also because they were expressed in an incomprehensible language. The individual sounds themselves gave the impression of being divine because of their strangeness, and so manifested magical power. Of course the missionaries of these strange religions spoke Greek, and Greek was also the language of worship. But allusions to the foreign origin of each religion were also very much in evidence. They rang with scraps of incomprehensible language and names. Great store was also set on the possession of sacred writings, now written in Greek, though most of them were really or allegedly translations of ancient texts, with fabulous stories told of their origin and transmission. Emphasis was also laid on the need to have special skill in exposition, and this increased respect for the text as well as for its expositors. But all this was done not to discourage anyone who showed an interest, but to arouse interest and to stimulate people to look behind the veil of the mystery, to become fully initiated, and themselves participate in the divine powers and capacities.

Exposition played a particularly large part in Jewish worship.

But even here, not only the intellect but the feelings also were appealed to, and indeed were further nourished by a liturgy rich in hymns and prayers. Even the Jewish service did not leave the eye unoccupied: the spectator's eye was caught and held by pictures on themes from the Bible and legend which helped to interpret the readings and sermons. The variety of speakers, particularly the foreign ones, ensured that the service itself was interesting and lively. Features which were obviously theatrical were used; there were even dramatic presentations. These took place even more in the services of other religions, doubtless on the analogy of the dramatic ceremonies of the Greek mysteries, though now related to myths and legends of the various missionary religions of the east.

It is a reasonable assumption, which can indeed be substantiated, that the aim of this compelling movement was directed away from fringe miracle working with its almost fairground character and entirely external power of attraction to a central core of liturgical life, to a direct experience of the divine powers conjured up by the religion concerned—to powers, that is, which were the prime movers of mankind, of nature, and of the universe. In other words, all these religions, and the missionary philosophies too, were aimed at a cosmic mysticism. This movement from the fringe to the centre was thought of as a closed circle. It was meant to bring the man who had been carried to the centre back to the fringe, that is, to make him at the same time into a missionary, even if only part-time. And this did happen to a remarkable extent. The cults were propagated not only by professional missionaries but also by amateurs who used the circumstances of their occupations as merchants, sailors, soldiers, and the like to propagate their religion and to foster contact with the existing congregations of their cult.

But the balance between the centre and the fringe could also be upset. I am thinking here not only of the frequent instances of superficiality, in which a man remained content with externals and did not get to the heart of things, much less still took up membership. I am thinking also of the other extreme, where the mystical element did not just have an inherent importance but became over-important and led to escapism and hostility to the world, thereby tending to create a closed community. Gnostic cliques of this sort sprang up for instance on the fringe of communities of the Jewish mission. It would be wrong to conclude from this that the missionary impulse became extinguished in these groups. Here too there was an intensive drive for membership. Moreover, these people felt themselves to be even freer to recruit members than normal missionaries who were tied to their specific religious heritage. These extreme mystics believed that they were already living in the world to come, free from all the bounds and restraints set by visible history. The gnostics were able to move about freely and search everywhere for like-minded spirits, in whom they discovered children of god who had originally been related to them, who wanted release, and had to be released from the deceits of the world so that they might attain to the reality of the divinity which had been inherent in them from eternity. The most important forms of propaganda in this case were revelatory speech and speaking in tongues, that is, the experience of the language of the heavenly world.

Finally, I would like to add that all these phenomena which I have described found expression in a variety of literary forms. An interest in literary publicity was an essential factor in propaganda. Only fragments of this literature have been preserved. Christianity indeed learned a great deal from the other missionary religions, above all from Judaism. But the pupil then outstripped and prevailed over its masters and then had no reason to preserve the opinions of its one time rivals in the missionary struggle. But because their propaganda was also edifying, some of it was preserved as edificatory literature. In addition, ridicule and hatred have very often kept alive the memory of the significance and peculiarity of the propaganda which they attacked.

15 Early Gnosticism

RUDOLF SCHNACKENBURG

In recent work on the New Testament and the history of religion, the phenomenon of gnosticism, or gnosis, has very much come to the fore again. Well into this century scholars talked just of Gnosticism, meaning by this a collection of Christian heresies which flourished particularly in the second and third centuries and were combated by early Church writers. Then through research into various bodies of writings like the so-called Corpus Hermeticum, the Coptic gnostic books, and the Mandean and Manichean literature further east, it became more and more apparent that we were dealing with an extensive movement which flooded the Hellenistic world, took on many guises, and probably went back to much earlier times. It may even have been akin to a sort of "world religion", as G. Quispel suggested in the title of a book, *Gnosis als Weltreligion*,[1] though that perhaps is going too far. At all events it is desirable to distinguish between the Christian heresy of gnosticism and the spiritual movement of gnosis itself. Christian gnosticism is then only a particular instance of the gnosis which assailed Christianity like a parasite, as it did other areas of contemporary religious and intellectual life. In fact, gnosis infiltrated Christianity intellectually and threatened its very essence. It was indeed able to grow and proliferate particularly luxuriantly on the soil of early Christianity.

The study of gnosis has been considerably encouraged and furthered by new literary finds. First, the Mandean writings, which had long been known, were made more accessible to the world of scholarship through good editions by M. Lidzbarski.

---

[1] Zürich 1951.

Then an English scholar, Lady E. S. Drower, took an active interest in the Mandeans who still survive in tiny remnants in Iraq and Iran and are an old gnostic baptist sect. Her good contacts with them enabled her to track down and publish other important texts. Many new texts relating to Manicheism were also brought to light from as far apart as Egypt and China, so that the provenance of the writings alone gives some idea of the world-wide dissemination and activity of the religious system of Mani, which is the most developed form of gnosticism. Finally, in 1945 came an important find of old gnostic documents in Nag Hammadi, about sixty-two miles north of Luxor in Egypt. It comprised thirteen codices, containing forty-nine gnostic works in Coptic, which for the most part had not been known before. These writings attempt to give the impression that they are more or less Christian products; but with not a few of them the Christian veneer is thin and conceals only slightly ideas which were originally gnostic. So in contrast to the picture of gnosis given by the Fathers, these Nag Hammadi texts, which are now gradually being published, represent valuable original documents which give us an insight into gnostic thinking and will keep us occupied for many years to come.

But what is gnosis, and what effect did it have in history? The first question, what gnosis is, can now be answered more accurately. The other question of its historical origin and influence is still obscure. But we must answer these two questions before we can consider the most important problem of all, which however is extremely difficult to solve, that is, the problem of the relationship between gnosis and Christianity.

"Gnosis" means "knowledge"—and in fact this concept stands at the heart of all gnostic thinking—but "knowledge" in a peculiar sense. As R. M. Grant says, it is "essentially self-knowledge, recognition of the divine element which constitutes the true self".[1] Its teaching is about man and his self-redemption. The gnostic asks about the origin and goal of his existence. As it says in an old quotation handed down by Clement of Alexandria, he is concerned with "who we are and what we have become; where we were and where we have been thrown; whither we are hastening, whence we are being released; what birth is, what rebirth".[2] We now have

---

[1] *Gnosticism and Early Christianity*, New York 1966.
[2] *Excerpta ex Theodoto* 78.2.

the same idea expressed in, for example, the so-called "Gospel of Truth" from the Nag Hammadi texts:

> He who knows is a being from above. If he is called, he hears, he replies, he turns to him who calls him, and he ascends to him. He knows what he is called. Possessing gnosis, he carries out the will of him who has called him; he desires to please him. He finds rest. The name of the One comes to be his. He who thus is going to have knowledge knows whence he has come and whither he goes.[1]

We learn more too from this. The gnostic talks of an "above" and a "below" and of an "ascent". The ground of his being, the divine spirit within him, originates in the heavenly world, a spark of light which has descended from the divine world above to the dark universe of death and lies hidden there within the gnostic. This is his true self. All efforts are now directed to releasing this inner being, the "self" of the man, from the entanglements of the material world, to bringing it back to the heavenly world of light and thus arriving at the essence of man's true nature. This is brought about by knowledge of being, by gnosis.

To illustrate and develop this anthropological doctrine of redemption, a mode of mythical and symbolic speech is brought into play. Because the gnostic thinks he can know being in its origin and because in his eyes the macrocosm of the world is related to the microcosm of man, a myth is first developed about the origin of the world, a cosmogony. It is intended to explain how the evil material world could have originated from entirely spiritual, divine being, and why man finds himself to be a being tied to a material body, ensnared by the passions and lusts of the senses and enslaved by the dark power of fate. It would be too much to go into more detail here about this myth of the origin of the world which circulated in a number of forms and modifications. We hear a great deal about aeons and emanations which are intended to explain the fall from the highest divine realm of the Ogdoad or the Pleroma by stages; we hear strange names of mythical figures and powers which alternate one after the other in a confusing sequence; we meet fantastic concepts and images. What it all amounts to is that man has fallen under the influence of evil powers but longs to escape from the remoteness, the alienation,

[1] *Gospel of Truth*, 22.

and the forlornness of this world and wants to return to his divine origin, to become divine again himself.

To this end a further myth is brought to bear which describes redemption. Often it involves a mythical redeemer figure who comes down from the highest heaven, is at first overcome himself by the deceits of the world, and is swallowed up in self-oblivion, as for instance the king's son in the "Song of the Pearl" or "Hymn of the Soul" in *The Acts of Thomas*. But a call from the heavenly world stirs him or a letter reaches him, he remembers his origin and his mission and, conquering the evil powers, he ascends victorious to his heavenly home. But this myth, which again circulated in a variety of forms, is only the outward form of what every gnostic experiences and strives after; it is only meant to give a picture of the redemption which he acquires through gnosis.

A further point is made clear by the gnostic myth: gnosis has a distinctive attitude to the world and to life. An attitude of this sort is the prerequisite of gnostic thinking and of the gnostic longing for redemption. H. Jonas has shown this in his work *Gnosis und spätantiker Geist*[1] by drawing out phenomenologically similar features in the numerous and bewildering variety of gnostic systems. The gnostic's understanding of man's life and self, which Jonas puts forward, seems in many ways very modern, even to the extent of the imagery. Being tossed into the world, dread, self-oblivion in stupor, sleep, or drunkenness, alienation, and yearning for the realization of one's true nature—all these ideas belong to the categories of gnostic thought and language. Even the way of redemption, or more precisely the recovery of one's true self (hearing the call which in gnosis does come from outside but in the last analysis means the call of self discovering self, and also the rejection of the phenomenal world, that is, becoming unworldly)—all these are not far removed from the existentialist understanding of life. The gnostic strives after release from the coercion of fate, after the true freedom which is to be found within himself. We can understand how in such a period it also became a sort of religion. So we should not be surprised that a gnostic attitude to life and the spirit is also to be found in philosophy. In particular, it is those schools of philosophy which are influenced by religion and inclined to some sort of mysticism, at that time Hermetic

[1] 1934.

philosophy, Platonism, and Neo-Platonism, which are related to gnosis or influenced by it. At any rate, it has not yet been definitely established when we should really speak of "gnosis", where the points of contact are, and where the influences came from. In this as in other questions we shall have to wait for further discussion.

The question of the origins of gnosis has been answered basically in four ways. First, there is the famous remark of Adolf von Harnack that gnosticism is "the acute Hellenization of Christianity". Like others he considered that the main factor in the formation of gnosticism was the Hellenistic spirit, or more specifically Greek Platonic philosophy. Secondly, within the history-of-religion school it was thought that the roots lay in the eastern religions. R. Reitzenstein had considerable influence with his thesis of an Iranian redemption mystery,[1] according to which there had already been an old Persian myth about the "redeemed redeemer". Alongside this, thirdly, the idea was held—and has continued to be held until now—that gnosticism grew out of Christianity, that is, that gnosticism was made possible by the prior existence of the Christian belief in a redeemer, however much certain intellectual currents may have paved the way for it. Finally—and this is a growing trend in the most recent research—scholars are inclined, as a fourth view, to locate the source of gnosis in heterodox Judaism. As we now see more clearly, Judaism, which has been so fertile religiously, was not confined only to the official "orthodox" line with which we are very familiar from the New Testament and from the great literature of Judaism, the Mishnah and the Talmud. It also included many special groups—Baptists and apocalyptists, Essenes and Qumranites, mystics and ecstatics. It is conjectured that it was particular groups like these, more inclined to speculation and mysticism, which were the creative source of gnosis.

What are we to make of all this? The first theory, of the acute Hellenization of Christianity, can today be regarded as obsolete. As long ago as 1913 E. Norden remarked in his famous work *Agnostos Theos* that we "might think that we were in another world when we look at this material, which really shares only its use of the Greek alphabet with the Greek way of life". The view held by the history-of-religion school—that an old Iranian myth of

---

[1] *Das iranische Erlösungsmysterium*, 1921.

the "redeemed redeemer" lies at the bottom of it all—has recently been seriously shaken by the researches of one of its own number into this school and its notion of a gnostic redeemer myth, Carl Colpe (1961). The idea that there was no pre-Christian gnosis, as the third solution asserts, was not convincing even earlier because of the Hermetic literature, and has now been almost certainly refuted by research into Mandaism and by the Nag Hammadi texts. On the other hand we must allow for a Jewish element in the origins of gnosis, as is suggested by many indications in the texts themselves and in the accounts of early gnostics. But the problem remains obscure, as H. M. Schenke established in two articles which appeared a little while ago in the periodical *Kairos*.[1] All the indications however suggest that the new attitude to life which is to be designated gnostic may have arisen in the medley of religions and peoples in the area of Syria and Palestine not long before the emergence of Christianity but independently of it.

In fact several converging observations point to this solution. Mandaism spread from the west to the east, as we now know for certain from one of the writings discovered by Lady Drower—the Haran Gawaita—and probably from the region of the Jordan. Simon Magus, whom we also hear of in the Acts of the Apostles, is named as the father of gnosticism by the Christian opponents of heresy. He came from Samaria and even after his death continued to have great spiritual influence. In various books of the New Testament, as we shall shortly see, false teachers are opposed who were obviously motivated by Jewish gnostic ideas. Most of them come from the area of Asia Minor, but the libertines attacked by the Epistle of Jude were probably from Syria, and the false teachers of Asia Minor may also have had their spiritual home here. The martyr bishop Ignatius of Antioch in Syria also betrays contact with gnostic ideas at the beginning of the second century, and the Odes of Solomon, coming from the first half of the same century, are most likely to have their origin in Syria. Egypt too was affected by gnosticism, but the area of Syria and Palestine still remains the most probable background.

It will be difficult to determine which heterodox Jewish circle contributed most to the development of gnosticism. R. M. Grant would account for gnosis from the disillusion which took hold of

[1] Vol. 7, 1965.

apocalyptic circles when their fervent hopes were not fulfilled. G.
Quispel points, with regard to the gnostic myth, particularly to
Jewish speculations about Adam which can be shown to exist in
various groups. R. McL. Wilson finds a noteworthy source in the
Qumran movement, whilst G. Scholem considers early Jewish
mysticism to be the seedbed. Probably all we shall be able to say
is that this "heterodox Judaism" was suitable ground for the
reception of gnostic strains of thought. For, since there is also
an immense Gentile element in gnosis, we cannot regard Judaism
as the sole factor in the gnostic movement. More likely it acted as
a catalyst in giving shape and efficacy to gnostic ideas. In any case,
the last word has not yet been said on this problem.

In many of the later writings of the New Testament ideas which
we come across and heresies which are attacked bear unmistakably
gnostic characteristics. We are here on hotly disputed ground.
There are tendencies in recent studies to see gnosticizing false
teachers and opponents of the Pauline gospel at work everywhere,
even in the early Epistles of Paul—that is, not only in the Epistle
to the Colossians, where this is more or less undisputed, but also
as early as the Epistles to the Galatians and Philippians. It is difficult to reconstruct from the attacks of the apostle the ideas of the
people whom he is attacking.

Of particular interest is the situation at Corinth, at that time a
flourishing port and meeting point between east and west, where
the most diverse minds—wandering philosophers, Jewish and
Christian missionaries, and the adherents of other cults—came into
contact with one another. Paul first combats false apostles coming
from Judaism in 2 Corinthians, opponents who attacked his own
apostleship and created an impression by their pretentious be-
haviour. But Paul had already tried in 1 Corinthians to put down
ideas in the Church which were opposed to his message of the
crucified and risen Christ. He battles against a false striving after
"wisdom" (2—3), against libertinism in sexual matters (6.12–20),
but conversely against a rigorist abstinence too (7), then once
more against a misdirected sense of freedom (8—10) and against
a denial of the bodily resurrection (15). Can these faulty attitudes
be traced back to one basic false attitude, to a common denomi-
nator? Recent work suggests that we also have to take into serious
account the fact that certain gnostic ideas, stimulated perhaps by
the experience of the Spirit (cf. 12), had found their way into the

minds of many people. Was a gnostic feeling for freedom and power springing up in the Christian Church at Corinth? Did they deny the future resurrection because they thought that the true, spiritual resurrection had already taken place for the man who was a gnostic?

We do in fact hear of such a view in 2 Timothy, with the names of its advocates (2.17f). It is also clear from other passages in the Pastoral Epistles that at the time of their composition Jewish gnostic heretics were confusing Christian believers with "godless chatter and contradictions of what is falsely called gnosis", as it says literally in 1 Timothy 6.20. This was an encratite movement, that is, one which showed its contempt for the body and for all matter by prohibiting marriage and the eating of many kinds of foods (4.3), and also indulged in mythical speculations (4.7; cf. 1.4). At the other extreme were the Nicolaitans who are mentioned in Revelation (2.6,15), who again were libertines, and who gave themselves over to sexual orgies and led others into joining them. Throughout the entire history of gnosticism we meet these two contrary tendencies of libertinism and rigorism. The dualistic denigration of the material led on the one hand to the idea that everything earthly is bad, and that sexual desire, pleasures of the palate, business, and wealth must be shunned and prohibited, and on the other hand to the contrary position which made light of these things that were meaningless to the gnostic, and encouraged a man to abandon himself to debaucheries and even to sin as much as possible, in order to manifest the spiritual power which was unsullied by them.

Other gnostics are opposed in the Johannine Epistles: christological heretics who were aspiring after knowledge of God, vision of God, and fellowship with God, but who rejected the Christian way of salvation. Jesus Christ for them was not the saviour who had come in the flesh; they believed that they could achieve union with God without him. They were indifferent to morality, not interested in keeping the commandments; they were particularly reproached for neglecting brotherly love. There is some indication that their propagandist activity and their successes were not inconsiderable. The heated defence and the credal statements presented in the Epistles clearly establish that we are dealing here with early gnostic heretics, although we cannot definitely reconstruct their teachings. They are similar to the docetists who are attacked in the Epistles of Ignatius.

But in this case, as in that of John's Gospel and of other New Testament writings, we are able to make an interesting observation. Although the early Church fought off the gnostic way of salvation with determination and principle, in the confrontation between Christianity and gnosis specific terms, categories of thought, and formulations of questions were also taken over. Anyone who argues with an opponent must find a form of speech which is intelligible to him, and must defeat him on his own ground. How far gnostic motives exerted an influence on early Christianity as it burst upon the Hellenistic world, and to what extent they impinged on the formulation of christology, is hotly debated. The claim that it was the so-called gnostic redeemer myth that first made it possible for the early Church to develop its full christology may be reasonably doubted on the basis of the latest work in the history of religion.

In any case we can see a tense struggle going on between gnosis and faith, between a doctrine of redemption in this world and inside man, and a biblical one of redemptive history, a struggle between myth and biblical revelation. There are scholars who think that the beginnings of Christianity in Egypt were impregnated with gnosticism. The fact is that a profoundly anti-gnostic work like John's Gospel was very soon seized on by gnostics and interpreted to fit their views. Origen wrote his own great commentary on John (which unfortunately has not been preserved in its entirety) against the first gnostic commentary of Heracleon. Gnostic "Gospels" from the discoveries at Nag Hammadi, such as the Gospels of Thomas and Philip, also teach us that the gnostics knew how to seize on the words of Jesus and fill them with a new gnostic meaning. They also produced a poetic literature, with works like the Odes of Solomon, unique in their character, rich in fantastic imagery, and certainly captivating for men of those days. The struggle between the gnostic world-view and the Christian religion was at its fiercest in the second century and reached another climax in the third century in the conflict with "Persian gnosticism", the extremely dynamic Manicheism. Mani, a Persian, devised a complete gnostic system from a variety of elements, and the Manichean "church" became an extremely impressive organization, as we know from Augustine among

others. Certain gnostic Manichean ideas have been at work under
the surface, occasionally appearing in all sorts of sects, right
through the Middle Ages until modern times.

That in the end the form of Christianity held by the Catholic
Church, critical towards gnosticism, won the day is not just the
result of external factors such as the power of the Church, the
skill of its leaders, and the intellectual vigour of its teachers and
writers. It was also a struggle between two attitudes of mind, between an anthropological doctrine of redemption created by man
and a religious gospel which offered man the salvation of the God
who stands over against him and demands faith and obedience.
In other words it was ultimately a battle between a pseudo-religion
and a faith which binds man to a personal God. Gnosis and faith
are two possible human attitudes, as we learn from history, which
a man must learn to distinguish and between which he must
choose.

16 The Influence of Jesus after his Death

HANS CONZELMANN

The subject "The influence of Jesus after his death" can be taken in two ways. On the one hand, we can take it in a purely historical sense—in which case it would be better expressed "The impact of Jesus. . .". This can be understood as parallel to the impact of a poet or philosopher after the end of his life and work, his power to make an impression after his time. On the other hand we can take it in the sense in which Christian faith takes it. In this case too the visible, historical impact of Jesus, the expansion and impressive history of Christianity, are part of the picture. But for faith this impact is due simply to causes within history. It is understood as the supernatural influence of the risen Christ who leads his Church —and not only his Church—in all its ways. The beginning of this influence which is "seen" by faith, is recounted by the biblical stories of the appearances of the risen Jesus to his disciples. In these he gives them his legacy: "Go therefore and make disciples of all nations" (Matt. 28.19). This gave the Church its direction for all time. And the risen Lord promises the Holy Spirit to his own as the power which enables them to believe and to overcome the world. He explains to them that even now—in fact now for the first time—he will be with them in a new way, "until the end of the world". This is the perspective of *faith*. It is to faith that the question is put—and has been put right from the beginning— whether faith does not rest on fantasy, on visions, on mythical patterns of thought.

How do these two approaches—the approach of history and the approach of "faith"—relate to each other? Do they exclude each other, do they stand alongside one another but without any connection, or can they positively complement each other?

Let us begin with the historical approach which is open to any-one to pursue provided he acquires sufficient insight into the facts. It is true that from the Christian side doubts are occasionally expressed whether this approach is really permissible. Jesus is said to be far more than a man—he is the Son of God. Any approach which treats him as a man is a consequence of unbelief and fails to grasp his true nature. On this we can make only two preliminary comments in the brief space at our disposal. First, Jesus is an his-torical person and the tradition about his life and work is deposited in historical documents. Secondly, you cannot ask for faith to be given in advance—first you have to believe and then you can learn something of the historical Jesus. Apart from the fact that according to Christian conviction faith cannot be generated by me but is a gift from God, the basic principle remains true that any-one can understand historical reports. For this, what is needed is not faith but knowledge of the subject. What faith can comprehend lies on another plane: that in the destiny of Jesus God himself and God's salvation for the world are to be encountered. This under-standing of faith goes beyond theoretical knowledge of history and the world. It extends into the realm of a relationship with this God today, who makes himself accessible in the figure of a man who was put to death.

If then we first talk of that impact of Jesus after his death in so far as it can be recognized in purely historical terms, we are talk-ing of it in the same sense as of other historical people. The "life-work" of Mohammed also includes the effect he had on the forma-tion and expansion of Islam. We are accustomed to say that a philosopher, poet, or creative artist has been "immortalized" in his work, and by this we mean that inspiration still stems from him to this day. This impact is dependent on many factors which can-not be checked. There are insignificant causes which spark off unexpected consequences. On the other hand, there is the un-expected genius who never "gets a turn". A historical person can, positively or negatively, be relatively understood or else remain a centre of controversy through the years. The interpretation can change suddenly from "Hallelujah" to "Crucify".

It is the appearances of the risen Lord which are the basic fact of the impact of Jesus. Whether or not one believes in his resurrection, the fact remains that a section of his followers quickly gathered again after his death and that these people appeared in public and declared that they had seen alive that Jesus who had been put to death. The whole of the expansion of Christianity is stamped by this experience. Success was not denied: Christianity became a "world religion" which determined the history of the West and exerted a powerful influence far beyond. It is true that, particularly in our world which is still strongly influenced by Christianity, we must bear in mind that historical success is no criterion for truth. Time and again we hear it argued that if Christianity were not true it could not have had this impact. This argument is both dangerous and unchristian. It is dangerous because it is possible to match every historical judgement with a contrary judgement. Right, Christianity was successful, but was the *cause* which Jesus stood for also successful? Has the world been brought nearer peace? What do we make of the fact that Christianity has made use of force, that untold numbers have been murdered in the name of Christianity? Try reading history through the eyes of the per-secuted—of the Jews for instance. And the argument is un-christian. If we argue from the success of Christianity, this means that to some extent we are spared the act of faith. The first Christians could not look back to success but only to the collapse of the work of Jesus. And when they looked into the future there was nothing to suggest world-wide success and power. But the problem goes deeper still. Precisely because of its world-wide success, Christianity must be prepared to answer the question: Was Jesus' ministry intended to make *this impact*, to have *this* sort of success? Does *he himself* occupy his proper place in the history of Christianity? Or has his work been distorted? Who was he? What did he intend? What is the relation between the Church and the reality of the human life and teaching of Jesus?

If we take as our starting point what we can establish from the Gospels to be the teaching of Jesus, clear lines emerge which lead from Jesus to the faith of the Church: belief in God, the Creator and Father, who lets his sun rise on the good and bad; the concept of man who does not come up to what God expects of him and yet who lives by his grace; the commandment of love which is so radically interpreted that it applies even to one's enemy; the expectation of the kingdom of God, of eternal salvation. We are not asking whether the Church has done justice to this teaching in its *conduct*. If it has not, then it will be judged by its own teaching. At all events, in this teaching the legacy of Jesus is preserved in the Church. But now we have to note that not all these lines lead directly from Jesus to the Church. They have, to use a metaphor, a "kink" in them, which is constituted by the death and appearance of the risen Lord. *After* this, his followers do not regard it as their foremost task to adopt Jesus' style of life— to "imitate" Jesus. And while they continue his teaching, they do not regard its preservation as the focal point of belief, but rather the public proclamation that Jesus lives, that his death is the salvation of the world, that in consequence salvation for time and eternity depends on acknowledging Jesus as Lord of the present and the future. They thus distinguish the influence of Jesus after his death *quite fundamentally* from just a faithful preservation of his memory and his legacy. They do not just teach that Jesus *despite* his death is a living power in the present because his teaching strikes us as impressive and binding. They teach rather that *through* his death his influence continues, in fact that his influence "today" is nothing less than the impact of his death on the cross, that the situation not only of believers but of all men at all times and in all places is determined by this death.

This connection of faith with the death of Jesus is so strong that a great part of early Christian writing shows no interest at all in the life of Jesus. In the letters of Paul there is not one word about it. Even the Gospels pick out from the life of Jesus only what throws light on his death. They do not, for instance, give any indication of what Jesus looked like. In the conviction of the whole of the early Church, the life of Jesus was completely orientated towards his death. As regards our subject this means that Jesus had an influence in history not because of his human legacy but because the Church worships him as the Son of God who became man and suffered death for the salvation of mankind, who was raised by God, and who now reigns over the world at the right hand of God. Christians know that this doctrine is bound to appear as "foolishness", because nothing of the power of this God and of the Son of God is visible in the world, except the impotence in which Jesus died and disappeared from the world.

This—the death and, above all, the resurrection—is the area in which modern theology now talks of "demythologizing", and where the Christian public has its doubts. For they have heard that not only opponents of Christianity but theologians too describe the resurrection of Jesus as a "myth". Paul's comment then seems appropriate: "If Christ has not been raised, your faith is futile and you are still in your sins" (1 Cor. 15.17). First of all, we need to ask what can be established as fact about the events after Jesus' death. To reach an answer we must once more refer to the stories of the appearances of the risen Lord, which we have already mentioned. It is they which bring about and set up both Christian belief and the Church. For if it is true that Jesus is alive, even if as a supernatural reality, then this truth must be declared to all the world. The appearances immediately give rise to mission. Mission is nothing less than the practical consequence of Christ's claim to supremacy.

Having ascertained this, we are still on purely historical ground. By taking an objective look at history we can see that the Church was founded by these appearances—or rather, bearing in mind the way our subject is formulated, that it was they which gave rise to the impact made by Jesus after his death. This fact can be verified by anyone from the historical documents. Establishing this still does not amount to a confession of faith. On the contrary, precisely at this point there is a parting of the ways. These stories cannot, of course, compel belief. The circumstances which they tell of can be given quite "natural" explanations. They can, on the other hand, be taken as literally true and still not evoke faith. The important thing therefore is to determine correctly the relation between natural explanation and faith. The generally accepted view on this seems to be more or less as follows: Either you take these stories to be true, in which case you are a Christian; or else you explain them in natural terms, as sheer inventions or as visions or hallucinations of the followers of Jesus, in which case you are not a Christian and may even have to be an opponent of Christianity. A Christian is, then, someone who believes in certain supernatural events in the world, as distinct from someone who relies more on his powers of reasoning. This is how the relation between faith and reason is widely presented, and by both sides— Christian and antichristian. And it is due to this that the argument between them has reached a dead end. For presenting the alternatives in this way makes them absurd.

Saying this does not mean that we are set on reaching an easy compromise in order to make faith more palatable by omissions. It means that, if we want to talk about this problem meaningfully, we cannot speak of "faith" in general and superficial terms only;

we must on the contrary give precise detail about what the general content of faith is, i.e. that God in Jesus has brought redemption into the world for unredeemed mankind and makes it available today and every day through the preaching of the crucified and risen Christ. This faith is "unreasonable" or beyond reason as long as it is not apparent to the world why God deals in such a way with it, giving to it so unreservedly. For this faith there is no other "factual proof" than the man crucified. If the opponent of Christianity argues that the resurrection of Jesus is not a historical fact, then the appropriate Christian reply is not "But it is", but "As a matter of fact you are quite right". This however might be understood to involve two concepts of "fact" and so obscure the position; it is necessary to give precise information about what we mean by "resurrection" and what constitutes its essence.

What do we mean by a "fact"? A state of affairs which can be conclusively demonstrated to everyone, which everyone, that is, can verify. But in this sense the "resurrection" cannot be a "fact". It contradicts the essence of the resurrection if it can be incorporated into the world, into the chain of cause and effect. This is not the way to arrive at the truth of faith. You cannot reach the truth without making use of faith *today*. The decisive question is not whether we can create for ourselves a distinct *image* of the resurrection of Christ—it can only be an image—but whether we today (just like many generations before us in history) can testify that Christ is Lord, that is, that he is the true standard for the world.

What then of the stories in the Bible of the appearances of the risen Lord? It is obvious that in those days men had a different picture of the world from ours today. That is true of both Christians and non-Christians. Heaven was conceived as the upper storey of the universe and the Ascension in consequence as an ascent in space. This is the conception, the picture of the world, which has been subject to change. But we must ask ourselves what is the point of these stories. Are they intended to "proclaim" a picture of the world as such, to make it the content of faith, or do they have a meaning which goes beyond the picture? The answer is clear enough: it would never have occurred to Christians in those days that the meaning depended on the picture of the world. For the picture was the same for both Christians and non-Christians. This is precisely where the difference from the present discussion lies. In those days it was out of the question that anyone should think it possible to have a particularly "Christian" picture of the world. The point of these stories, which is in fact perfectly clear, is something quite different. When they talk of "heaven" they mean the state or "sphere" of salvation which puts an end for ever to evil in the world. They proclaim that Christ is alive, that God is with men. But how? In the way which can be seen on the cross of Christ.

To sum up: what appears from the outside to be a defect—that there is no objective proof for the truth of faith—is an advantage for faith itself. For we have here more than a series of striking miracles. We have the disclosure to the world of its salvation. What is actually visible is the crucified Lord, the man Jesus, whose life's work had manifestly failed. Come to understand him as the bearer of eternal salvation, as the opportunity of gaining standards for distinguishing between force in this world and peace in the world to come, between death here and life there, then you will grasp that God has raised Jesus from the dead—in other words, you will understand the influence of Jesus after his death.